(Photo: Aamer Mitta)

ABOUT THE AUTHOR

Susan Viets reported for the *Guardian*, the *Independent* and BBC World. She has also contributed to CBC, *Newsweek*, *USA Today*, the *Moscow Times* and other publications. She lives with her husband in Toronto.

PICNIC AT THE IRON CURTAIN

PICNIC AT THE IRON CURTAIN

A MEMOIR

*From the Fall of the Berlin Wall to
Ukraine's Orange Revolution*

Susan Viets

DELFRYN BOOKS
DELFRYN PUBLISHING AND CONSULTING INC.

ISBN: 0987966405
ISBN 13: 978-0-9879664-0-7

Cover design: Cai Sepulis
Map graphic: Haley Anderson

AUTHOR'S NOTE

Many people in these stories have kindly given me permission to use their first names. When I was unable to reach someone, I used a pseudonym to protect that person's privacy. I compressed timelines in some chapters. Chapter One stretches over two years. I met the women on the ward at different times, as I recovered from different operations. Chapter Four compresses two visits to Chernobyl. I first went with Swiss scientists in August 1990. My second trip was with Volodymyr Shovkoshytnyi in April 1991.

Picnic at the Iron Curtain is based on diaries, reporting notebooks, letters and memory. Chapter Ten relies heavily on news articles. These are listed in the Sources section.

Many of my friends read the chapters in which they appear, provided details about events that I described and helped catch mistakes. I struggled with the spelling of place names, particularly Kiev. The transliteration from Ukrainian is Kyiv but the more common practice is to write Kiev, so I used this spelling.

CONTENTS

NORTH SEA
BALTIC SEA
GERMANY
Berlin
AUSTRIA
Vienna
CROATIA
Zagreb
HUNGARY
Budapest
Sopron
BOSNIA & HERZEGOVINA
Sarajevo
ROMANIA
Bucharest
MOLDOVA
Chisinau
Tiraspol
Odessa
UKRAINE
Kiev
Chernobyl
L'viv
BELARUS
Minsk
RUSSIA
Moscow
Zaporozhye
Mineralnye Vody
Grozny
BLACK SEA
KAZAKHSTAN
ARMENIA
Yerevan
AZERBAIJAN
Baku
CASPIAN SEA
UZBEKISTAN
Khiva
Tashkent
Samarkand
TURKMENISTAN
Ashgabat
KYRGYZSTAN
Bishkek
Almaty
TAJIKISTAN
Dushanbe
Qurghonteppa
CHINA
AFGHANISTAN
IRAN
ARABIAN SEA
MEDITERRANEAN SEA
MAP OF KEY LOCATIONS
500 km
500 mi

I

LONDON

I first travelled to the Eastern Bloc because of an accident in October 1986. I was hit by a truck while cycling in London and received a small settlement from the driver's company. When Canadian friends visited me in hospital I described the truck. It weighed 16 tonnes and was part of a demolition fleet. I told them that the truck had rumbled too close behind as I biked home from my class at the University of London. My basket brimmed with jars of salsa, fresh chilies, tomatoes, black beans and all the other ingredients for tacos. I do not remember the moment of impact even though I remained conscious as it happened. I landed on my back on the sidewalk near Euston station. Clouds swept overhead. I stayed still for a while and then tried to prop myself up on my elbows, momentarily distracted by a bright green door across the street. Its brass knocker glinted in the sun. Groceries lay scattered on the ground. An ambulance arrived from Emergency. Paramedics took charge. As I told the story to British friends and relatives, different words slipped in. I was struck by a lorry, rode a push cycle, landed on the pavement.

An ambulance attendant offered a gas mask. I resisted. She said, "Love, you'll enjoy it. It'll be like downing ten pints." I next remembered a door swinging open at the University College Hospital Casualty Department. Then I woke up on the orthopaedics ward, in a cast from ankle-to-hip.

I was horrified when the surgeon explained that he would soon drill holes in one of my shinbones (I imagined him wielding the type of Black and Decker that lay in my parents' garage) and install hardware to keep shattered bits of bone in place. A few days later when he next operated I was so high on painkillers that I felt quite calm. As I recovered, I became chatty in my drugged state and I made friends with other patients. Days passed, then weeks, and we bonded. Mrs. M., who had the bed directly opposite mine, sensed a romantic catastrophe.

"No letter from him again dear?" she inquired one day when she saw a stack of mail on my bedside table. I did not want to discuss it, so I just shook my head.

Most of Mrs. M.'s body lay hidden from view, swaddled in hospital sheets, just like mine. I could make out a large, lumpy figure and blue tinted hair. Mrs. M. had regular habits in hospital that included afternoon tea at three o'clock.

"Care to join me for a cup?" she always asked.

"No thanks," I would answer.

She insisted that day, so I said yes. Mrs. M. sent a friend over with a porcelain cup. It contained a generous quantity of scotch.

Beside my mail stood a stack of university course books on the history and politics of Eastern Europe and the Soviet Union (I was studying for an M.A.), and a pile of magazines that chronicled current developments in that part of the world. I read all day and learned that Hungary – that small country on the edge of the Soviet Bloc – was one of the boldest to experiment with reform. Confined to bed, unable even to reach the bathroom, I travelled in my imagination as far as Budapest. I did not know how I would get there or when, but I wanted to visit Hungary to see the changes that had occurred first-hand.

Mrs. M. remembered Hungarian refugees who had fled the Soviet invasion thirty years earlier, in 1956. "I saw some of them at Paddington," she said. "The poor dears they looked so lost, leaving behind their homes. Who knows what horrors they saw." I wondered what she thought of all that time in bed. In my hospital cocoon the outside world receded and I dreamed.

Money helped turn those dreams into a plan. Another ward neighbour, Edith, who could not hear, delivered the good news. Edith usually wore a hearing aid in each ear. However, as she was ferried from another hospital to this one, both devices had disappeared. Anyone who wanted to talk to Edith had to shout.

Early one day Edith stood over a locker between our beds. She clutched envelopes.

In a loud voice I said, "Good morning, Edith, that's my mail."

She did not turn in my direction or respond in any other way. Instead, she took one letter and opened the envelope.

"Someone's written from a legal firm. It's about money," she bellowed. Then she picked up her large white-rimmed magnifying glass, peered and shouted out the contents of the letter. I had won a small settlement from the trucking company for the accident.

The news spread quickly. Patients in nearby beds congratulated me. If she'd been there I'm sure Mrs. M. would have said,

"When we're out you'll have to buy us all a round," but she was not. She had disappeared in a bed shuffle. The ward was like that. Beds filled and emptied with no warning at all.

A few days after I underwent another operation, I noticed a new neighbour, a small and slender woman in her early eighties whom the nurses called Moira. She stood by her bed holding a pair of scissors and asked me if I would help take the hem down on her pink nightgown. I wondered how to respond to this unusual request. I told Moira that I would be happy to help but that I could not get out of bed because of my leg injuries. She shuffled over and gave me the scissors; I undid some stitches. Then I heard Moira call out, "Porter!" The surgeon, on rounds with his students, stopped.

Moira said to him, "Porter, please take my bags. I'm ready to check out."

I put the scissors down and hoped that no one noticed the unpicked hem. Moira climbed back into bed. Really, though, I felt like her, ready to check out and get my life rolling again.

About a month later, a nurse appeared with a pair of crutches.

"Those are for me?" I asked hopefully.

"They are. It's time for you to stand," she said. "That's all we'll try today." I shook from the effort because my muscles had atrophied.

"Don't worry," she said. "You'll be walking again in no time at all." She was right. Within days I hobbled down the ward and back again. I visited bedridden friends. My confidence grew. Soon I was ready for discharge and my first steps on the street.

Dogs were afraid of the crutches, so they barked at me. The hardware that protruded from my leg repelled and fascinated people. Strangers always stopped me to ask questions about it. Happy to be free, even though I could not yet move far, I planned. I had already missed many classes and with more operations scheduled, would have to postpone exams and extend my M.A. for another year. Now I had time on my hands. I used it to audit lectures external to my course work so that I could learn more about Hungary.

The Hungarian prime minister visited London. A professor who specialized in Hungarian politics took me to the press conference for the prime minister and his delegation. It was held in a stately room, packed with bright lights, televisions cameras and journalists. The buzz and energy contrasted vividly with the quiet libraries of academia. This life seemed much more dynamic and fun.

The professor introduced me to a BBC reporter stationed in Budapest. I told him that I wanted to visit Hungary, watch the demonstrations, see all the change.

"Get journalistic accreditation," he urged. "Anyone can watch protest marches but only journalists have access to senior leaders in the Hungarian government, press conferences, Parliament."

"How?" I asked. He pulled out a pen and scribbled down a list.

"That's what you need to do."

In the weeks that followed I thought about what he told me and decided to act on his advice. I telephoned foreign editors at newspapers to inquire about the possibility of reporting for them in Hungary. Although I did not have experience, some editors expressed interest because I knew a little about Communist Hungary at a time when few others did. Through a friend in Canada I obtained a letter from a news agency.

Vaguely worded, it only said that the agency might take occasional reports, but it was printed on letterhead, a criterion for accreditation. That letterhead, and the editor's freshly inked signature, made my heart leap.

The day finally arrived for my last medical appointment. I sat in the crowded waiting room at University College Hospital. When the receptionist called my name I hobbled into the orthopaedics clinic.

The doctor examined a recent X-ray and said the bones had healed well. I could not thank him enough. The metal bar and screws that protruded from my leg had already been removed. Now I could walk without crutches, which meant I could travel with ease. This excited me the most. I knew exactly where I would go.

I landed at Budapest Ferihegy International Airport in May 1988, with press accreditation for a Communist Party conference. I asked the taxi driver who drove me into the city a question in Russian.

"That language, people will spit at you," he growled in one angry burst of Hungarian-accented Russian.

I sat in silence for the rest of the trip, partly cowed by the driver, but mostly dazzled by the stately Austro-Hungarian architecture. Parliament buildings stretched along the Pest side of the Danube River; elegant bridges arched over it. Then there was the spectacle of the castle district opposite, perched high on the Buda side. We passed people at an outdoor café that overlooked the river. I had not imagined such scenes or beauty in a Communist country.

The next morning I arrived at the conference venue. "We won't sit with the delegates? I so wanted to see Kádár," I told a Dutch reporter as an organizer corralled us in to the press centre, far from the conference hall. The reporter did not answer but just slid away and kept her distance after that.

I filed stories that no one commissioned,

"But it's historic. Károly Grósz just replaced János Kádár as General Secretary of the Communist Party," I told the Ottawa news editor in my most persuasive voice.

"We took it from the wires," he replied.

None of my stories was published, but I did not mind at all. Just sitting in the press centre, pounding telex keys convinced me that I was already a journalist.

After the conference I met with a Foreign Ministry press officer who promised me permanent accreditation. Certain more than ever that luck ran in streaks and that mine had turned, I now focused on finding a rental apartment. After rummaging through a language school garbage can, I found an ad for an apartment in central Budapest. Luckily it was still available and the landlady spoke English. She accepted a deposit. I flew back to London on a wave of optimism, my accident in the past, convinced that Hungary would undergo significant change. I planned to return in a few months and felt that nothing could go wrong.

2

EAST GERMANS

One Sunday morning in July 1989 I heard the doorbell ring. I looked down from my second-floor kitchen window and saw three enormous knapsacks and the tops of three heads, no one that I knew. I was now a stringer for the *Guardian* and had been thrilled to receive business cards that stated Budapest Correspondent in bold type. I hesitated for a moment before going downstairs as I was at work on a story. When I opened the door, a young woman with a strong German accent and short blond hair held out her hand.

"Sabine," she said, then quickly added, "I know Jonathan. He gave me your address."

Sabine asked if she and her two friends, Helga and Ute, could stay with me for a week.

"We are from East Germany and the biggest problem for us in Budapest is accommodation because we have not enough money to live in hotels."

I had hosted many visitors, though none from the Eastern Bloc. I respected my English friend Jonathan's judgment. If he had sent Sabine, she must be trustworthy. I already admired her straightforward manner and adventurous spirit. She and her friends did not let financial constraints stop them from travelling and exploring. I hoped faced with a similar situation that I would behave the same way.

I guessed that Sabine could be no more than a year or two younger than me. She wore tidy no-name jeans, a T-shirt and comfortable walking shoes – a practical choice for someone small perched under such a large, heavy knapsack. She had an open likeable face, with an easy smile. I told Sabine and her friends that they could stay.

"We are thanking you so much," Sabine said. As we climbed the stairs to the apartment, Sabine informed me of her itinerary in Budapest.

"We will first visit the castle district," she said. "We know that the district is rebuilt after heavy damages in the war."

Sabine's friends, Helga and Ute, had not yet spoken. They followed behind. Once inside the apartment, Sabine took charge. She instructed Helga and Ute where to place their belongings. I stood aside and watched.

There were hints this was no ordinary visit early on. It seemed rude to ask what my three East German guests carried in their tractor trailer–sized knapsacks. They unpacked and the kitchen shelves soon overflowed with pots of dried noodle snacks and other instant meals from East Germany. They did not pitch tents on the living room floor, but otherwise had all the supplies for an urban camping expedition. None of the dozen visitors who had stayed with me over the past few months travelled like this.

It was late afternoon by the time they finished, so I offered to make dinner. Helga hovered near the kitchen door.

"May I help?" she asked. I handed her a small paring knife and a few tomatoes.

"Thanks," I said. "Could you chop these?"

Helga sliced each tomato into perfect, identically sized wedges. Her movements were spare and her physique, lean. Taut in face, body and manner, she seemed a serious, pensive nineteen-year-old. As we sliced vegetables, Helga discussed politics. She spoke in a low, intense voice, which indicated she was someone with strong opinions but with enough experience not to share them widely.

"There are really great differences between the situation in DDR and Hungaria," Helga said. "We heard a lot about the changings in Hungaria and I want to see this for myself."

I told Helga that I did not know much about her country but had heard the East German government was repressive.

"I can understand why you're curious about political developments here," I said. "That's what drew me to Budapest."

I told her about key events that had occurred since my arrival nine months ago – demonstrations that began as opposition against a huge planned Gabčikovo-Nagymaros dam project along the Danube River fuelled more political protest. Support for opposition parties that demanded a market economy and democratic elections grew quickly. Reformers in the Communist Party backed such change and seemed better aligned with opposition groups than with hard-liners in their own party.

"We hear that the old guard is being shaken off and everyone began to speak about all kinds of problems. This does not happen in DDR – why so late for us?" Helga said.

Over dinner Helga, Sabine and I chatted. Ute remained quiet. She spoke very little English. At times she stared intently as she tried to follow the conversation, but for most of the meal, she ate slowly, absorbed, I thought, in her own world. She had big eyes and long hair that draped down over the back of the chair. If Sabine was the boss and Helga the thinker, Ute was the dreamer.

I told my East German guests that in London people called Hungary "the happiest barracks in the camp."

"This is good," said Helga, "and maybe DDR is the unhappiest barracks." Everyone laughed, even Ute, after Helga translated for her.

We discussed Hungary's aggressive reform experiment and wondered whether an order from the Communist Party or interference from Moscow would abruptly reverse the changes. They did not offer an opinion. Both Sabine and Helga seemed interested in Hungary's progressive Communism.

"I would like to get to know how you think, because you follow events from another perspective," Helga said.

I described my initial impressions of Hungary, surprised that life here differed so much for the better from my expectations. My mother had visited Leningrad a few years earlier – an elegant city she said, filled with dour citizens dressed in drab clothes. The Soviet Bloc loomed in my mind as one large monolith and I therefore assumed that Communist Budapest would be similarly bleak and foreboding. It did not take long for these preconceptions to change.

Helga interrupted. "Yes, but you knew people from Hungaria and how it must be?"

"No, I didn't know anyone here."

"Just like us," Sabine quipped.

"But I felt at home almost right away," I said, "though, I had no idea how much Hungarians despise the Soviets."

"We do not hate Russians in the DDR," Sabine said. "They're ahead of us. I try to teach some of what I learned in Moscow in my classes but I am not allowed. It is too progressive for us."

"Hungaria is different, the happiest barracks," said Helga. "In countries like Poland you have always to wait in long lines for something." She glanced at Sabine.

I said that the Hungarian Communists surprised me. I never expected reformers in the party to lobby so aggressively for change, though the political opposition generated the freshest, boldest ideas. Many of the opposition members spoke English, so I could talk to them without an interpreter. Law students, about my age, vibrant and intellectually sophisticated, founded a liberal, reform-oriented political party, Fidesz. I went to their meetings, barbecues, parties and wished that all this existed at home. I never thought that I would be jealous of students in a Communist country. I told the East Germans that I wanted a life like this too.

"I had a crush on one of the opposition members, but not anymore," I confessed. "Shotsy, the man with the megaphone. He leads the Fidesz marches." They giggled.

"Handsome?" Sabine asked.

"Lean, energetic, this fiercely determined sense of purpose," I replied. "We had drinks together after a massive demonstration that ended at the central television station. I asked Shotsy how he felt as he stood at the top of the steps, with tens of thousands of protesters at his feet."

"I knew if I told them to charge the building, they would," he said.

"Those opposition leaders have so much power but they're restrained," I told Sabine and Helga. "I guess that's why the change is so orderly."

Two events stood out for Ute, Helga and Sabine: the first, the April 1989 initial withdrawal of Soviet tanks from Hungary. Two months later the government cut through an Iron Curtain section in Hungary, which left a big hole in a barbed wire fence that separated Hungary from Austria, and the Soviet Bloc from Western Europe.

"Liberation," I started to say. Sabine interrupted, her interpretation, different:

"When the tanks went and the cut in the Iron Curtain happened people in DDR thought our leaders would lock the border," Sabine said. "We wanted to come to Hungaria before the locking."

I imagined gigantic impregnable gates slamming shut all around the border of East Germany. I could go anywhere in the world that I wanted. Travel options for Ute, Helga and Sabine, already limited, were about to become worse. They would soon be prisoners in their own country.

"The problem how to pay the holidays is not easily solved," said Sabine. "Our leaders only let us change a little bit of money for the currency of Hungaria. When this is spent we must go home."

Sabine told me that she had planned a holiday in Budapest while it was still possible. Her younger neighbour in Dresden, Ute, asked if she could come. Ute's university friend, Helga, joined Sabine and Ute. They carried food from East Germany and asked to stay so they could save money and prolong the trip. I felt embarrassed that we had used their supplies for dinner. I would have to stock the fridge.

The four of us managed well in a small apartment. Sabine and I shared the bedroom. Ute and Helga slept in the living room. By remaining tidy, we could still manoeuvre even though their backpacks occupied half the space.

Sabine had a list of must-see sites. During the day, if I did not work, I led my East German guests on these trips. We wandered through cobblestone streets in the castle district and rode the funicular, with its panoramic view of the city, back down to the river bank. We had tea at Gerbeaud's in Vörösmarty tér. Inside, time stood still. This spacious coffee house with high ceilings and no trace of Soviet influence attracted many in the city. We lounged on wicker chairs with green cushions. People nearby read newspapers or talked in small groups. Most seemed settled in for the day. Chandeliers hung overhead. We lingered and sampled pastries.

One rainy evening, we had drinks at a local bar, the Fregatt. With its wood panelling and low lights, it was as cozy as the dry, warm lower deck of a ship. I bumped into English and Hungarian friends. The band played. We listened a while, then talked politics and gossiped about friends' relationships. When I next looked round, I saw Ute in the distance surrounded by young guys in jeans and blazers, that prosperous, stylishly bespectacled look of Bohemian West Germans. Ute, different now, animated in her own language, laughed a lot. Later that night as we lay asleep in our beds, male voices woke us. The West Germans stood on the street by the apartment and shouted for Ute.

Seven days passed quickly. Sabine packed her knapsack for the trip home to Dresden. Ute and Helga asked if they could stay a few days longer.

"No problem," I replied. I enjoyed their company.

We took Sabine to the train station. When we returned home, Helga, so serious again, said, "We must speak."

I put the kettle on for tea and then carried the cups through to the living room. Helga sat in one armchair, Ute in another. I perched on the sofa. A small coffee table with a vase of pink bougainvilleas stood between us. Steam rose from our mugs of tea.

"Ute does not want to return home," Helga said. "She wants to go to West Germany." Ute watched. She and Helga spoke briefly in German.

"Will you help?" Helga asked. "Ute has an uncle in West Germany. He'll support her."

I was stunned and felt foolish. Earlier in the week a friend had joked that I harboured refugees and I joked right back that I had nothing more clandestine than tourists at home. I was so focused on Hungarian politics that I did not notice the big news in my own apartment.

"Does Sabine know about this?" I asked.

"No," said Helga.

I wondered about the dynamic between Helga, Ute and Sabine. I could not imagine travelling with a friend, even a neighbour, and concealing such significant plans. Maybe inclusion would jeopardize Sabine's situation in East Germany, or they might just not trust her.

"Are you going as well?" I asked Helga.

"No, I will return home in some days," she said. "There will be suspicions if I do not go soon." I wanted to help them, but what they asked might mean breaking the law. I felt confused and needed time to think.

"So why are you going back?" I asked Helga.

"I thought about leaving with Ute," Helga said, "but the best place for me to make changings is at home."

She would join an opposition group in East Germany, one that opposed the Communist regime and protested against environmental degradation. Helga hated what she called "disinformation" in university lectures. Humiliated, she said, "You don't know the feeling to be a second-class human being everywhere and every time because you can't pay with hard currency." Such honesty was compelling.

I wondered whether Ute had discussed escape plans with her parents but did not like to ask such a personal question. I just asked why she wanted to leave. Ute simply said, "I don't feel free." Our conversations, so halting and broken because of language difficulties, meant that I never really knew Ute. I felt a stronger affinity with Helga, who would not remain long.

I was distracted during Helga's last days in Budapest and did not know what to do. Helga and Ute had discussed the escape plan in private and once divulged, began to act on it. I still wondered if escape was a good idea.

Helga and Ute had only seen the good side of Hungary. I felt fairly confident that the reformers would win but could not forget one incident the previous autumn that showed a dark side of Communism still lurked in the system.

A small group of Hungarians had planned a demonstration, a march to the Romanian embassy. They would give the embassy staff there a petition that protested Romania's treatment of ethnic Hungarians resident in Romania. Sallie, who was an established journalist from London, would cover the march. I worshipped this friend. She epitomized the best in journalism. She was professional, objective and brave with a good code of ethics. The foreign press corps in Budapest remained tiny – no more than half a dozen reporters – so we spent a lot of time together, which served as an informal apprenticeship for me. If she covered the demonstration, I would too.

We met up the road from the embassy where the protesters gathered. The crowd numbered no more than a few hundred people. The organizer made sure that everyone stayed on the sidewalk so traffic flowed well. Then we began walking down the road toward the Romanian embassy. Sallie and I positioned ourselves near the front of the crowd.

I heard people shout *rendorszeg* [police]. Policemen on motorcycles appeared. Their motorcycles flanked us on three sides. We stopped, trapped between the motorcycles and buildings that lined the sidewalk. Then, through a gap in the rows ahead of me, I saw more riot police with plexiglass visors and shields. They rushed forward and I heard dull thuds as their thick black truncheons struck backs, arms, legs. People in front screamed and pushed their way back to escape. In the confusion, Sallie and I were separated.

I noticed some people held handkerchiefs over their faces. Then my eyes stung. The police had used tear gas. I turned and hunched down, saw a gap between buildings and an alley. I pushed and jostled through the crowd, reached the alley and ran faster than I imagined possible. I ducked into a basement café and rinsed my eyes in the bathroom. Then I stood by a tiny window and looked up at the street. I saw people's feet as they ran past and then the black boots of policemen who chased them. I ordered a coffee. My hand trembled as I picked up the cup. I hated the police and the government that ordered police action. What had commanders told the men behind visors that made them attack with such vengeance?

I wondered how Ute would be treated if she were caught at the border. I worried but did not discuss the situation with anyone else in case it compromised Ute's efforts to leave or her future in East Germany, if she returned. East Germans who tried to escape could still be imprisoned; in the past, border guards sometimes shot them. I trusted two people – Sallie and Anna, a Hungarian friend whom I met through my landlady. Both Sallie and Anna were away on holiday.

I respected Anna's judgment. She also made me feel safe and secure. Every morning I took Buda-bound public transport over the Széchenyi bridge and walked the short distance from Moskva tér to Anna's apartment. I crossed through a courtyard and entered a quiet world shielded from the bustle of the street, and then into her apartment. Anna usually hovered over the kitchen sink when I arrived. Often she cleaned dirt from vegetables that soaked in a pan. She boiled water for coffee, put cups on a tray with a plate of cookies and we would walk through the dark hallway into the living room.

Natural light poured in from massive windows that faced the street. Anna's daughter, Juli, a toddler, usually sat on the floor with toys. Sometimes Anna's husband, Gyula, and their six-year-old son, Dani, would also be home. I loved it there. Anna's family was my surrogate family for those two years in Budapest.

Over coffee, Anna helped me read the Hungarian papers. She had a sharp mind and good news insights. I looked forward to our morning conversations and wished that Anna was in Budapest so that I could ask for her advice on Ute's situation.

When Helga left, I felt responsible for Ute. Had someone told me a year earlier that I would help an East German escape I would not have believed it. This would abuse my position as a journalist and breach trust with the paper that sponsored me. It might also be illegal. Most people born in the Eastern Bloc knew many laws made no sense and broke them to survive. Ute's request sent me down that path, though I felt that I might lose something of myself along the way.

I could see that Ute remained determined not to return. Ill-informed about the situation in East Germany, I did know about some difficulties she would face as a refugee. That winter, I had spent time in Budapest with a twenty-six-year-old

Romanian refugee named Victor. We met under a hotel awning in heavy rain. As we waited for it to stop, Victor told me his escape story.

Victor's girlfriend, a member of the Romanian Securitate secret police, worked in the passport office. Victor persuaded her to get him a passport for what he said would be a short holiday. He stuffed school certificates, which could not be taken out of the country legally, down his trousers and ditched his tour group when he arrived in Hungary. I felt appalled that he betrayed his girlfriend so casually but also admired his resourcefulness and courage, traits common in many refugees that I met. One of his friends swam the Tisza River twice to escape from Romania. He was shot at, apprehended and imprisoned the first time, but succeeded the second.

As I came to know Victor and his friends I observed their lives in Budapest, struck by their vigilance, which verged on paranoia. They believed that the Securitate operated in Budapest and kept them under surveillance. Victor never returned home through the front door. He always entered via a back courtyard and climbed in a window to shake off anyone who might tail him.

Would Ute have to live like this? I did not and could not discuss it. Our lack of a common language meant that we still communicated on the most rudimentary level only. In some way, after all this time together, we remained strangers who shared an apartment. I needed someone trustworthy to bridge the language barrier. I telephoned a student, Zsolt. He sometimes translated Hungarian for me. He also spoke German. Zsolt had a square build and scratchy goatee and was helpful and reliable. He came over immediately.

When the bell rang, I ran down.

"Thank you so much," I said and explained the situation as we climbed the stairs.

"She will be caught and thrown in jail. It will be a disaster," said Zsolt.

I couldn't deny this possibility but also discounted Zsolt's comments given his predisposition for pessimism and hyperbole. Often when we attended demonstrations, Zsolt insisted that security service agents were following us and might arrest us. Such intrigue appealed to his imagination. I enjoyed Zsolt's company despite this focus on doom.

Zsolt sat in the armchair that had been Sabine's favourite. He grimaced when Ute explained her predicament and ran his hands through his lank blond hair. Zsolt and Ute spoke to one another in German. I only understood the word "Stasi," the name for the East German secret police. During their brief conversation, Zsolt mentioned the word "Stasi" at least six times.

"Let me think about the situation," Zsolt said. "I'll telephone someone with connections tonight."

I did not press him for details.

Zsolt arrived at 9 a.m. the next morning. When I let him in he said, "I saw a car with unmarked licence plates parked outside. The driver's watching your entrance." I didn't respond.

"You're being monitored by the security services." Normally I acknowledged his latest espionage theory and then changed subjects, but today such speculation disturbed me. I did not want to hear it. We sat around the coffee table. Zsolt pulled an ink-blotched sheet of paper from his bag with a telephone number scrawled across the top.

"A border runner's co-ordinates," he told me in English. Then he translated and told Ute that for a fee, the border runner would take her to fields by the Austrian border near where

Anna and I saw a portion of the Iron Curtain dismantled and lead her from Hungary into Austria at a remote and, he claimed, rarely patrolled location. A risky option, I thought.

As Ute absorbed the information, Zsolt detailed pitfalls in the plan. The border runner would flee with Ute's money, leaving her destitute and stranded. A bleak assessment, but I sensed Zsolt's full engagement and that he would help Ute escape.

Another option emerged. Ute often spent time in a neighbourhood adjacent to the West German embassy. Reluctant to approach the embassy, she thought that East German security agents photographed everyone who entered, so they could identify potential East German escapees. On her outings, Ute met other East Germans, also "on holiday" in Budapest. The West German government allowed East Germans West German passports. Some of the people that Ute had met applied for them inside the West German embassy. Since they knew they could not obtain an exit visa from the Hungarian government, which they needed in order to leave Hungary for a Western country, these East Germans declared themselves refugees once inside the West German embassy and refused to leave the embassy grounds. Ute opted for this tactic.

A line of like-minded East Germans now stretched down the road by the embassy. An official gave Ute a number and said she should return in three days for her embassy appointment. She felt nervous because she had seen men on nearby rooftops who photographed people in line.

I tried to distract Ute. She liked bars, especially the Fregatt. We went back. Once there, I suspected that she had bar-hopped earlier in the trip to find a Westerner who might marry her to help her escape. A day before her embassy appointment we returned home from the Fregatt around midnight. I turned the radio on. The BBC news reader said that the West German embassy in Budapest had now closed its doors to East Germans, citing overcrowding and unsanitary conditions. This, despite assurances from embassy officials that they would review Ute's case. What a betrayal. I told Ute. She panicked. I also felt on edge.

In the morning Ute called the border runner. She had considered telephoning before but didn't want to. Now she felt desperate. As they spoke and planned an escape, Ute lost confidence and trust in this man, abandoned the plan, and returned regularly, instead, to the West German embassy. East Germans in a similar situation congregated there. One day Ute came home with Agnes, an East German student. I thought of Agnes as a substitute Helga, a friend of Ute's who spoke English, though Agnes, like Ute, lived the nightmare of trying to escape. Zsolt and I were mere witnesses to this predicament.

I could pick Agnes out in any crowd by her mass of frizzy hair that stuck up on end. Bold by nature, she had already tried to cross the Austro-Hungarian border three times. On her last attempt she tripped a wire one and a half kilometres from no man's land. Border guards with dogs came after her. One guard fired a shot in the air. Such warnings were allowed, but shooting anyone trying to cross was not. Agnes might have escaped if she'd run but she was so scared, she stopped. The guards warned her against making another attempt. They said twice as many patrols would soon reinforce the border. The guards drove Agnes back to Budapest. Like Ute, she did not know what to do.

The West German and Hungarian governments began refugee crisis discussions. In mid-August, the Hungarian Maltese Charity Service opened a refugee camp in Budapest. Finally someone stepped in to take charge.

A few days after the camp opened, Ute, Agnes and I sat in the living room and discussed options. Ute said, "The camp is quite good." I had not visited the site.

Agnes said, "Many people have already moved in. Perhaps we will go."

I watched as Ute gathered her belongings. She folded and then rolled her clothes in compact bundles that she tucked in her knapsack. The shower curtain rack, draped these past weeks with damp laundered T-shirts and underwear, now lay bare. Her sleeping bag, now as familiar to me as my bed-spread, hung in a tight roll strapped to the bottom of her bag. Ute checked documents, clutched her passport, hoisted that heavy pack on her back. Then Ute, Agnes and I walked down the stairs.

"I'll visit you," I said.

"We are thanking you so much for your hospitality," Ute replied. Then they stepped across the threshold, into the street. I felt as if I had thrown helpless refugees out the door. I woke the next morning worried about Ute and Agnes. I needed to know they'd be okay, so I went to the camp.

It was situated on spacious grounds surrounded by a wrought-iron fence in an attractive residential neighbourhood. Tents stood everywhere. Refugees sat scattered among the flow-erbeds. Some lay on towels with backpacks at their feet. Others stretched out on the grass. Portable latrines and small cabins dotted the landscape.

I broke the rules by entering the camp, but no one noticed as I still looked like a student. I met some families with chil-dren. Most of the refugees were young and single, like Ute and Agnes. Money was tight for many, but at least they now had free accommodation and food. Still, everyone seemed understand-ably stressed as they found themselves stuck in limbo. They worried about the repercussions for relatives in East Germany because of their decision to leave, and they remained desperate for a way out of Hungary to West Germany.

A few days after Ute and Agnes arrived at the camp I received a faxed notice about a pan-European picnic organized by a descendant of the last Austro-Hungarian emperor, Otto von Habsburg, and a Hungarian opposition group, the Hungarian Democratic Forum (MDF). The picnic would be held a few days later at the Austro-Hungarian border, near Sopron. I phoned for more information. Organizers planned to temporarily open a rural border post, closed for years, for a pan-European friendship meeting between neighbouring villagers on opposite sides of the border. Dignitaries and journalists from the Hungarian side would travel to the Austrian side in a bus through the border post for celebrations in Austria.

What an opportunity. I immediately went to the camp, found Ute and Agnes and discussed a picnic plan. The site was an area near the breached Iron Curtain. They had given up on escape but that now seemed a possibility again.

Early in the morning on the day of the picnic I went to the car rental agency. The agent handed over keys for a rickety-looking Lada, the gear shift loose. I wondered whether we would break down along the way. Then I picked up Ute, Agnes and Zsolt. The picnic was not scheduled until later in the afternoon. We arranged to arrive early, ahead of the organizers. We needed time to explore the back roads near the site where we hoped to find a remote, patrol-free crossing where the Iron Curtain used to be.

We followed the directions sent by the picnic organizers. We found ourselves in a field near the border but did not know where the border actually lay. No signs marked anything. We stood, surrounded by fields bisected here and there by dusty country lanes. As we explored further, hoping to find a sign post, we noticed occasional cars parked haphazardly along the roads or in fields, all of the cars, two-stroke engine East German Trabants. Eventually we found an abandoned guard tower. A cluster of people stood nearby. They spoke German. Ute, Agnes and Zsolt chatted with them.

"They're looking for the border," Zsolt told me.

"Maybe we'll see it from the top," I replied, pointing at the guard tower. Zsolt and I climbed the tower. From the top we spied people in small groups. East Germans, we thought. They wandered up and down lanes for miles around. We could also now see dozens and dozens of parked cars scattered through fields.

Hours passed. No one that we met had found a route to Austria. Now early afternoon, Zsolt and I went to register for the picnic and the bus ride over the border. I pulled out my press accreditation. The woman at the registration table looked at it.

"The *Guardian* — a wonderful paper," she said. She asked how long I'd been in Hungary and had a few other questions. Then she handed me a flimsy square of paper stamped with the word *sajto*, which means "press."

"Will they check passports at the border?" I asked.

"No, this is all you need," she said and pointed at the stamped paper. "No other documentation is required for the trip."

I stepped away from the table. My heart thumped. My throat was dry. I knew that I needed to take two of those passes for Ute and Agnes.

I stood in the grass near the table and watched as another person registered. The woman in charge seemed distracted, but I could not bring myself to take the passes. Minutes ticked away. Then someone else registered. The third time I moved forward. The press passes stood stacked in a pile near the edge of the table. While the woman dealt with someone else, I took two and walked away. I felt sure that someone would notice, chase after me and take them back. No one did. I showed Zsolt the passes. He broke out in a grin.

We found Ute and Agnes and gave them the papers. They seemed happy, though guarded. I think they had already experienced too many setbacks to feel hopeful. We asked them to follow us onto the bus but not say anything. German chatter might attract suspicion. We boarded early. More people arrived. I watched anxiously as the bus filled, worried that there would not be enough room and that the organizers would realize more people sat in seats than had actually registered. After about half an hour no one else had boarded and several seats were still empty. The driver closed the door. The bus lurched down a narrow lane toward the border.

Within minutes it stopped. Zsolt and I sat near the back. From our window we could only see fields. We did not know what caused the delay. Ute and Agnes sat a little farther ahead. The driver opened the door and got out. Everyone followed. We saw that abandoned Trabants blocked the lane. Ute and Agnes had good instincts. They walked down the road. Then they started to run. We saw them pass a metal barrier that we thought must be the border. Other people ran. Ute and Agnes disappeared. A pack of East Germans raced down the road. Then everyone was gone. After all these weeks, Ute and Agnes had finally escaped. Zsolt and I stopped. We snapped celebratory shots at the metal barrier with my last frames of film. I felt a pang of regret as I realized that I had no pictures of Ute and Agnes. I had taken them for granted and thought they'd always be there. The end had come so suddenly.

Then Zsolt chatted with a Hungarian man who stood nearby. The man told us the border crossing lay farther up the road. We grabbed our bags and ran. Soon we saw one overwhelmed border guard. People cut through fields and bolted behind him. Others who were bolder, ran in front, beyond arm's reach. The guard did not stop anyone. I even thought that I saw him smile. It was a human stampede. Later I found out that more than 600 East Germans had raced by foot into Austria. Ute and Agnes long gone, I wished them the best in my heart and then crossed into Austria to interview as many people as I could find.

I stood on the dirt road, the dry earth disturbed by so many trampling feet. The air smelled musty. The sun illuminated floating specks of dust. Brown grass, desiccated by the summer sun, rustled in the breeze.

During one interview, I sensed that someone was staring at me from behind. At first I ignored this sensation. Then I turned. Agnes and Ute stood on the road waiting for me. I stopped the interview and ran over, yelled for Zsolt to join us.

"We wanted to come back to say goodbye," Agnes said. "There is a tent up the road with food and some people who help us. They'll find Ute's uncle."

My throat tightened. I could not believe that we stood together in Austria, Ute and Agnes finally safe. Not wanting to linger, they soon walked back up the road, farther into Austria. Zsolt and I turned in the opposite direction, crossed back into Hungary and drove to Budapest.

East German refugees flooded into Hungary. The crisis escalated. More refugee camps opened. The Austrians waived visa requirements for East Germans, but the Hungarians still did not allow them to leave. One day in early September, news leaked that the Hungarian government would open the border the next day and let East Germans out. Early in the morning I went to Ute and Agnes's old camp. More journalists arrived. Someone set up a table on the lawn and put a television on it. I stood in a good position. The crowd of journalists grew. Not long after, a news presenter read a statement that the border was now open for East Germans.

People in the camp applauded. Some cried from happiness. I wanted to whoop with joy, hug people that I knew in the camp, but instead stood aside and recorded what I saw.

Children on a hillside waved Hungarian and West German flags. Then people ran and packed their belongings. Many families had camped in cars. Their interiors were strewn with blankets, bottles of water and food packages. Young guys painted the West German flag on cars. Others who feared the decision could be reversed just left.

A friend and I drove to the border, the highway north from Budapest to Austria, a sea of Trabants. People sang; passengers hung out the windows. At the border they cheered the guards who waved them through. For hours we stood and watched a steady stream of cars go by. Then in the early hours of the morning we drove back down the deserted highway to Budapest.

A week later I received my first letter from Sabine, who still lived in Dresden. By then she knew of Ute's escape. I thought that I detected a note of bitterness in her letter when she wrote, "*I was so busy that I couldn't be sorry for Ute.*"

Then I realized that Sabine missed Ute. "*She {Ute} started to study now again. I hope the best for her. Sometimes I can't believe it and it's also difficult for me to stay alone in Dresden.*" I thought of Sabine and Helga and the others who had stayed behind in East Germany and wondered what would happen next.

Soon I received a letter from Helga. She wrote that Ute was now studying chemistry in a town near Munich. Life in East Germany, Helga said, was turbulent. For several weeks people in Leipzig and Dresden participated in massive protest marches against the East German government. The protesters clashed with the police and the government imposed travel restrictions on East German citizens. Helga joined an opposition group that demanded political changes including free elections and economic reforms. She later wrote that *". . . the situation was really bad and sometimes I asked myself if it was the right decision to stay in the GDR {East Germany}."*

I heard about these demonstrations on the radio. Some reports said that nearly 100,000 people marched at a time. I tried to imagine such huge crowds in narrow European streets, the possibility of tear gas and batons being used against them, but so many who demonstrated week after week was very bad news for Communist rulers.

* * *

On a grey Thursday morning in November, my clock radio alarm woke me, as usual, with the BBC news broadcast. The announcer said the Berlin Wall was being dismantled. I sat up in bed startled. This Wall that cut both Berlin and Germany in half was the ultimate symbol of the divide between communism and capitalism, Eastern Europe and the West. I could not believe the Wall would fall. I wanted to be there. Ute later captured in a letter what this event meant for East Germans. After her first walk from East Berlin to West Berlin she wrote, *"you can't imagine the feeling when I stood at last in this part of my home I never was allowed to go!"*

I washed and dressed quickly, impatiently waited for public transport over the Széchenyi bridge to Moskva tér and Anna's apartment. I arrived at 9:30 a.m. Anna and I swapped information in the kitchen and then she danced her way into the living room, as she celebrated the news. I followed behind, mugs of coffee in hand.

I tried to concentrate on the newspapers but felt distracted. I wanted to be in Berlin but had to stay put due to work obligations. Anna helped me develop a plan. If I took the last flight to East Berlin on Saturday night and the first back on Sunday, I could squeeze in a trip between assignments.

Helga lived in Berlin but left no telephone number for her university residence, which might not even have a phone. I would have no time to find her, but would just go to the Wall and spend the night there. I did not want to waste my few hours in Berlin on sleep.

I reached Checkpoint Charlie late at night. People laden with shopping bags streamed back from West Berlin. Laughter filled the air. There were so many happy faces and such exuberance on the West German side. It was one huge party at the Wall. That evening workers dismantled a section of the Wall at the Brandenburg Gate. With such crowds on the West German side, I could not actually see, so I stayed in East Germany for a better view.

East Berlin was nearly deserted and seemed spooky. Beyond Checkpoint Charlie, I only bumped into a few stray tourists, including a figure skater and his coach. We walked near the Brandenburg Gate and saw a gaping hole in the Wall, an entire section gone. Armed East German border guards still patrolled the area. They scowled. I wanted a piece of the Wall as a souvenir, so I moved closer to pick one up. One of the guards said something to me in German that I did not understand. Then he pointed his gun in my direction. I stepped back.

I continued to receive news from Helga. Ute was reunited with her family. She and Helga spent New Year's Eve celebrating under the Brandenburg Gate. Helga visited Ute in West Germany. Both now understood the size of the discrepancy between the two Germanys. Helga wrote that at her university in East Germany, "*. . . we as students have to learn to fight for our rights now. . . . Some of the biggest problems are the bad living conditions in the dormitories, the old equipment in the laboratories, bad lectures, the low level of language education, too less money and so on. It was interesting and a little bit depressive to compare our conditions with those of Ute's student life.*"

I received my last letter from Helga in early 1990. She had changed universities and would soon study at the Technical University of West Berlin. She invited me to visit and offered to guide me through both sides of Berlin. She said that she now knew the Western sector well. I felt tempted, but already had my sights set on a trip in the opposite direction, farther east, into the Soviet Union.

3

KIEV

On an early June evening in 1990 nearly one year after Ute, Helga and Sabine had arrived at my apartment, I stood on a platform at the Keleti station in Budapest waiting to board the train to Kiev. A group of friends came to see me off. After the last hug, I turned to step up rusty metal rungs into the train carriage. I heard a friendly voice behind me shout, "Behave yourself in the Gulag. I hope we see you again."

I entered the carriage, and a new world. A worn red carpet stretched down the train corridor. I walked through the narrow passage to my compartment. I slid the door open. Faded cream-coloured curtains hung across the bottom half of the compartment window; the air smelled of dirty mop water. I faced four bunks. Mine was the top right-hand berth. I climbed up and stowed my bags away. I lay down and did not look out the window. I thought that I might change my mind about moving to Kiev if I saw my friends still by the train. I already missed them.

I heard the door slide open and shut my eyes, pretending to sleep. I was not yet ready to meet my cabin mates. A couple, husband and wife, and one other man settled in, speaking softly in Russian. The husband mumbled Tanya and something about bags.

"Ivan, leave the food on the table," Tanya said. "Where's the vodka? Don't forget the pickles." Ivan and Tanya did not know the second man, who had the bunk opposite me.

The train pulled out of the station. Budapest receded. We clickety-clacked down the track, the train swaying soothingly. I relaxed, my mind free to wander in a way it had not been able to since my time in hospital. I thought of Ute and remembered what she had said when I asked her why she wanted to escape – "I don't feel free." She built a new life in West Germany. I headed in the opposite direction, toward the centre of her old world. Anna's husband, Gyula, had warned me that in this part of the Communist Bloc I might feel the same as Ute did. "The state will be your enemy," he said. "It will control where you sleep, what you eat and when you leave." I felt a pit in my stomach, a yawning chasm of worry as I thought back on those words. At the time, I dismissed them as exaggeration.

All that fear, anxiety and loneliness that accompany a new start crept back now – feelings that had been sealed away amid the excitement of planning for the move, the sense of possibility and potential. I thought that my test trip to Kiev a few months earlier had been successful. By chance, I had arrived in Ukraine at a time of major change, when a handful of members of the umbrella opposition movement, Rukh, just learned that they had been elected to the local Parliament, a small fissure of opposition MPs in an otherwise monolithic Communist legislature. I met with Ukrainian Foreign Ministry officials to request a visa and press accreditation. The request set a precedent as Ukraine was still part of the Soviet Union. There were no foreign journalists based in Kiev; they were all in Moscow. I received verbal support from Foreign Ministry representatives but after all these months had still not received the necessary documents. To move to Kiev with no certainty of accreditation was a risk. I clung to the idea that a promise is a promise but that pit in my stomach warned otherwise. At least I had made one acquaintance on my test trip, Yaroslav. He would be there to meet me at the train station and had found accommodation for me in Kiev.

I heard shuffling below. The couple in my cabin arranged items on a small side table by the window. They stood up.

"*Mushchina* [man], *dievushka* [girl], sit with us. We invite you to join us for something to eat," Ivan said.

The man across from me jumped down from his bunk. I hesitated for a moment. Then I followed. The two of us sat side by side on the lower bunk across from the couple. Square-jawed, Ivan looked fit and tidy with his short cropped blond hair and clipped moustache. Tanya, paunchier, assumed the role of genial compartment hostess. Both wore matching shiny tracksuits, flip-flops and socks. They looked as at home on board a train as they might be in their own living room. We introduced ourselves. Ivan handed us shot glasses filled with vodka. Small plates of bread, pickles and Ukrainian kovbasa sausage stood on the table. This was my first experience of Ukrainian hospitality.

We drank and ate. I answered questions about Canada, England and Hungary. Then tired and foggy-headed from the alcohol, I excused myself and climbed back up onto my berth.

I unfurled a sheet that lay neatly folded at the end of my bunk. It had been washed and pressed but had gone grey and limp with age. I thought that a Western rail company would have retired such a sheet from service long ago. Still, I appreciated the housekeeping effort. If my train ride was anything to judge by, Ukrainians might be poorer than most people that I knew in the West, but they were welcoming and certainly knew how to have fun. I slid under the sheet fully dressed and pulled a blanket over top.

Some time later Ivan woke me. "Take your suitcases down," he said. "We're near the border. The guards will want to inspect your bags."

I fumbled in the dark to retrieve my luggage. Ivan lifted it down to the lower berth. I followed and sat with my cabin mates. For a long time we heard clanging and banging as workers adjusted the train wheels to span the wider Soviet rail gauge.

Guards boarded the train. They wore military caps and uniforms with hammer and sickle insignias. They were unsmiling and unfriendly.

"Passport," one demanded. I handed my documents to the guard. He studied the visa. I felt nervous because Rukh had sponsored it. The organization, which had only recently acquired official status, campaigned for Ukrainian independence, a direct challenge to Soviet rule. Soviet authorities considered Rukh to be suspect and full of trouble-making renegades.

The guard examined my passport photograph for a long time. I did not know where to look when he stared at me. Direct eye contact might be interpreted as insolence, so I gazed off to the side. The guard finally handed the documents back and left the cabin. I climbed onto my bunk and fell asleep. The next day was a blur of more vodka, lots of jokes, some very bad music, tea from the train wagon lady, glimpses through breaks in the forest of stout women in headscarves and boots walking along dusty roads, blue and yellow Ukrainian flags in western towns, Soviet Ukrainian red and blue flags as we moved east and more broken sleep. Then, right on schedule, the train pulled into the Kiev station at 3 a.m.

I saw Yaroslav before the train stopped. He held a bouquet of roses in one hand and clutched the handle of a huge trolley designed to carry freight with the other. It was the only trolley in the station. I wondered if Yaroslav had to fight someone for it. People dragged bundles along the platform. Friends and family members greeted them with bouquets of flowers.

"Welcome to the nearly independent republic of Ukraine," Yaroslav said. He handed me the roses. Then he led me toward the exit.

We picked our way through the dimly lit station trying not to disturb anyone. Travellers sprawled across the floor nestled against oddly shaped bundles held together with rags or frayed bits of rope. The station looked like a refugee camp. I was glad not to be alone.

Yaroslav was slender and had a shock of blond hair. He was quick in all his movements and quick-witted too. At the age of twenty-one, he spoke Russian, Ukrainian, Polish, English and French fluently. He studied economics and also wrote and edited articles for the English-language news service for Rukh. I felt grateful to Yaroslav for importing me into Ukraine. He had persuaded Rukh leaders to sponsor my visa when I tired of waiting for papers from the Foreign Ministry to arrive.

On the road outside the station Yaroslav stuck his arm out and flagged down a car. It turned out that this was not an official taxi but rather a regular car driven by a man who had dropped a friend off at the station. Yaroslav and the man haggled over a price. I watched and learned. This informal taxi system – a glorified form of hitchhiking – seemed the best way to travel. Once Yaroslav was satisfied with the price we got into this car. He told me that anything, even an ambulance or a snow plow, could be a taxi if the price was right.

Our driver straddled lanes, flying through Kiev streets at top speed. I wondered if he had ever taken driving lessons. Fortunately the roads were deserted, so it seemed unlikely we would have an accident.

"Not very many people here own a car. You need good connections to get one," Yaroslav said.

He told me the names of the streets. We travelled down Taras Shevchenko Boulevard, turning left onto Khreshchatyk Avenue. Yaroslav also provided commentary. He said that the yellow brick buildings flanking the road were a reminder of Ukraine's bloody history. Parts of Western Ukraine had at various times been absorbed into the Polish, Austro-Hungarian, German and Soviet Empires. After the Second World War, brigades of German POWs constructed the buildings lining Khreshchatyk, including the main post office in the central October Revolution Square. As we passed the post office, Yaroslav asked the driver to slow down.

"See that entrance facing the square," he asked.

"Yes, what's so special about it?"

"The portico collapsed a few years ago. Everyone standing underneath was killed. The POWs got their revenge," he said. "Actually a lot of buildings here are poorly built and badly maintained, so watch out where you stand."

October Revolution Square spanned both sides of Khreshchatyk. A red granite statue of Lenin dominated the side of the square opposite the post office. I lost my bearings but could tell by the bumpy ride that we travelled up from the square along a cobblestone hill. We passed by the Golden Gate. Yaroslav said that it marked the boundaries of the ancient city, Kyivan Rus', which pre-dated Moscow and was a major centre of religion, trade and learning. We continued another block along Yaroslaviv Val. Then the car stopped in front of a building and we got out. Even in the inky darkness I could tell that it had once been magnificent but had crumbled through years of neglect. Yaroslav's cousin lived in the building but was away, so Yaroslav had arranged for me to stay in his apartment.

The light socket in the archway leading into the courtyard had no bulb. "They're always stolen," Yaroslav explained. Then he warned me to watch out for a large pothole that I could not see for lack of light. It was even darker inside the building. I dragged my hand along the wall to guide myself down the hallway. Once inside the apartment Yaroslav flicked a switch. "They mix chalk with the paint," Yaroslav said. "Don't lean against any of the painted walls unless you want your clothes to turn blue."

The apartment was dingy, with peeling wallpaper in the living room. However, it was well situated. Yaroslav explained that I could walk to the city centre from here. I thanked him for his help, then he left. I unpacked several rolls of Hungarian salami and smoked cheese and cartons of juice. The fridge did not work, so I stacked the food in the kitchen cupboard. I picked up the telephone receiver. I heard a dial tone. I went to bed, satisfied that I had a functioning phone. The next day I began my descent into paranoia.

In the morning I had an appointment to meet Yaroslav at the Rukh headquarters, near Parliament. I looked forward to this meeting as an opportunity to learn more about the organization's political manifesto. Rukh fought for independence, but I had not been able to uncover its plan for governing if this goal were achieved. All the political propaganda stressed the republic's wealth as the breadbasket of Europe, but said nothing about energy poverty that left it totally reliant on Russian oil and gas imports. I also wondered what Rukh's plan was for Ukraine's share of the Soviet nuclear arsenal and whether it would shut the Chernobyl nuclear power plant that had caught fire and exploded with such devastating consequences four years earlier, in 1986. At that time I had sat in my parents' den in Ottawa watching television news reports as neighbouring countries began to detect clouds of radiation and raised the alarm.

I walked down Khreshchatyk Avenue, past the Dnipro Hotel, to the Rukh office. I stopped to use a bathroom along the way. I opened the cubicle door and faced a cracked, stained toilet bowl with no seat. The floor seemed worryingly slick. A small plastic container mounted crookedly on the wall contained torn bits of newspaper instead of toilet paper. I felt certain that cholera lurked in the cubicle. I soon learned that when nature called it was best to take the tram to Parliament and use the clean bathroom there.

I entered the Rukh office and saw Yaroslav, who was busy at the fax machine, sending out his latest edition of the news. A tall, slender student, with the prominent cheekbones of a model, counted megaphones. The student locked the megaphones away in a cupboard and then turned and introduced himself. "Sashko," he said. "Those are our most important weapon," he added, gesturing toward the cupboard with the megaphones. Soon older members who led the organization arrived.

They welcomed me to Ukraine and showed me a desk where I could work. I did not speak Ukrainian, so I chatted in Russian, asked my questions but realized from the answers that no detailed policy platform existed yet. I thanked the Rukh leaders for their hospitality. I sensed tension and unease throughout the conversation. When the older men left I asked Yaroslav what I had done to offend them.

"It's the language," he said. "Some of them spent years in labour camps for writing poems or singing songs in Ukrainian. They've paid quite a price to keep the language alive."

I had studied Russian and Soviet history for five years and knew none of this. My crash course in history from the Ukrainian perspective had begun. I felt a sense of déjà vu from Budapest. I would not be able to speak Russian here and would need to hire a Ukrainian interpreter. In the meantime I sat at my desk and kept my mouth shut. Yaroslav told me that one leader asked him if I was *nashyi* [ours].

"What does that mean?"

"Whether you're with us or against us."

This was the language of war. I felt upset to be viewed with suspicion and also by such extremes that allowed for no middle ground as an impartial observer. I realized too that this situation was my own fault. A Rukh-sponsored visa came with expectations. I would need to break the tie to maintain independence. I was beginning to feel very alone in Kiev. In this city I had no family members, friends or colleagues, and knew no one of common nationality or mindset. For the first time I began to understand what it meant to be an alien. This struggle was about the right to exist as a Ukrainian and I was not one, so I almost did not count. I sat quietly in the office and listened closely to Ukrainian chatter around me, hopeful that I might soon absorb the language, or somehow feel more at home. Around noon I turned my attention to a new set of concerns.

I had a meeting scheduled that afternoon at the Foreign Ministry press centre with Mr. C. and Mr. I. We had met in March, when I requested accreditation. I had spoken Russian there and no one seemed to mind. What troubled me was that

I could not think of a good excuse to explain why I had arrived on a Rukh-sponsored visa, instead of waiting for government papers. Since I spoke poor Russian, perhaps I could play dumb and attribute the change of plans to a language misunderstanding. Something about Ukraine was turning me into a child prepared to tell any story to avoid getting in trouble. I would not behave this way at home.

I left the Rukh headquarters and walked up the hill toward Parliament. A wooded park, at the top of an embankment, ran alongside the road. The Foreign Ministry press centre was situated on a side street lined with trees, in a low rise nineteenth-century stone building painted pale yellow. A decorative knee-high metal fence ran along the front of the building. Flat oval-shaped street lamps hung from wires strung across the road. I did not know what to expect from the meeting, so I dreaded going in. I stood on the sidewalk and procrastinated a while. I stared at attractive brick apartment blocks across the road and wondered who lived inside. The buildings had bay windows and balconies made from finely wrought metal work. They were designed with care. Then I stepped up to the main entrance and into the press office.

Mr. C. and Mr. I. shared the office. Each sat at his own desk. Mr. C. was small, greying and stout. Mr. I. was large and imposing with jet black hair and big teeth. We chatted politely. They inquired about my trip. Then I gave them the letter from my editor (I now worked for the *Independent*) formally requesting press accreditation in Ukraine that had already been faxed to them at least a dozen times.

Mr. I. took the letter. He said, "*Solnyshko*, we will do what we can to help you but you are operating in a grey zone." He lectured me, alluding to the fact that I had made a mistake by coming to Kiev on a Rukh-sponsored visa, though never saying this outright. He ended by calling me *solnyshko* again, which means "sunshine." I was encouraged by *solnyshko* and even happier when I saw Mr. C. take a parliamentary press pass from his desk drawer and write my name on it. I felt so relieved. I was not accredited yet but a parliamentary pass meant that I would have freedom to work in Kiev.

"You will move into a foreigners' compound when you are accredited, just like the ones in Moscow," Mr. C. said. "We hope you will be the first swallow of the new season."

It surprised me that Kiev had a foreigners' compound because as far as I knew no other Westerners lived in the city other than a French consul general and a German consul general, both of whom had their own residences. I asked where the compound was located.

"It doesn't exist yet," said Mr. C., "but we will build one."

Mr. C. and Mr. I. took me into the room next door, where some journalists and Members of Parliament had gathered for a meeting. I peered out tall windows framed by sash curtains and admired the well-maintained antique furniture. A dozen people sat around a table in the centre of the room. Mr. C. introduced me. I lost track of names after the introduction to Vadym Boyko, a television reporter and MP. I tried not to stare. I could not fully concentrate in the presence of such a dramatically handsome young man. He had raven black hair, pale skin, red lips, a slender build and a perfectly still face, like a sphinx. He offered to show me the local television station where he worked the following week.

When the meeting finished one of the older journalists, with blue eyes and a weathered face, Slava, invited me for coffee. We strolled down the hill toward Khreshchatyk and then walked to October Revolution Square. Some of the chestnut trees still flowered. White blossoms lay scattered on the sidewalks and streets. The trees provided cover for birds. Kiev had little of the din of normal urban traffic. We heard birds singing in the branches and breathed in fresh, smog-free air.

People crowded the sidewalks along Khreshchatyk and October Revolution Square. They dressed perhaps not fashionably but very tidily, the men in neatly pressed trousers and shirts and the women in well-ironed skirts and blouses. In the square a group of women in headscarves and bulky dresses struck up a four-part harmony.

"Are they part of a choir?" I asked my colleague, Slava.

"Those *babas*?" he said. "They're just passing time." I had never heard such sonorous and moving songs from amateurs. We walked uphill along one of the roads that led out of the square and reached a building not far from mine.

"Just wait here," Slava said.

"Aren't we having coffee?"

"Of course. I'll get it now." I stayed put while he joined a line of people standing in front of what appeared to be a small opening in a wall. I saw no chairs or tables or glass-fronted façades that might indicate the presence of a coffee shop. Twenty minutes later Slava returned with two chipped teacups filled with brown liquid. We stood on the corner and sipped the brew. It looked like coffee but tasted oily and bitter.

"Are you hungry?" Slava asked.

"A little," I said. I did not like to complain about a lack of food, even though I had so far found little in Kiev. Earlier, Yaroslav and I had gone into the Dnipro Hotel hard currency bar for a snack. We bought one small bottle of mineral water for $US5 and equally overpriced Snickers bars, past their due date and covered in a waxy white film. I decided not to eat mine but regretted this now.

"Wait here. I'll be back in a minute."

Slava went into a small building with a sign that said *gastronom*. He soon reappeared with a bag full of ginger cookies shaped like miniature hubcaps. We ate a few.

"Please, take the rest with you."

"Thank you, they're delicious." I would not normally eat a bag full of cookies but wanted them in case I found nothing to eat later on. We said goodbye. Slava strolled down toward the square. I decided to go to the *gastronom* to try to buy food for dinner.

The window displayed no items, which is probably why I had not noticed the store before. A large woman in a white lab coat stood behind the counter. Enormous jars of pickled tomatoes filled a mesh wire bin in the centre of the store. The shelves were bare and the store, empty.

"Do you sell any food besides tomatoes?" I asked the woman.

"*Nyet*"

"Do you have milk?" The woman grew impatient. "*Dievushka*, I just told you we have nothing else," she said. "If you want milk, go to a milk store."

I held up the ginger cookies and asked if she had more of these. She became very angry and told me to leave. I was being thrown out of a grocery store for trying to buy food.

At least I now understood how to identify a grocery store. My eyes properly trained, I eventually spotted the word *moloko* [milk] and found a milk store. It was also empty. This store did not even have a cash register. A woman in a white lab coat and tall white chef's hat stood beside an abacus with big black and brown wooden beads.

"Do you, by any chance, have milk?" I asked.

"*Dievushka*, of course not," she shouted. She paused and looked at me for some time. Are you a foreigner?" she asked. I explained that I had only just arrived in Kiev.

"Come tomorrow by about 6 a.m. and you should be in the line early enough to get some milk," the woman said. I left the shop.

I had never encountered food shortages in Budapest. The supermarket near my apartment was always stocked to capacity. But it unfortunately sold products with unilingual Hungarian labels and no pictures to provide visual clues as to the content. The first time I shopped at the supermarket I bought one of each item that appeared to be food. At home, if the dictionary provided no appropriate translation, I snipped open the packages to taste and identify the contents. I managed not to sample anything poisonous. Here, even though everyone on the streets looked well fed, I could not find any food to taste. I would have to ask Yaroslav for help.

I walked home convinced more than ever that Communist Kiev and Communist Budapest had nearly nothing in common. I wondered whether my move here had been rash and worried that I might not be able to manage in Kiev on my own. I decided to call the foreign editor to let him know that I had arrived safely and to give him my phone number. It would be comforting to hear a familiar voice. I dialed the international operator to place the call. She asked me the day and time for the booking.

"I'd like to make the call now, please," I said.

"Impossible," the operator said and hung up. I phoned the operator again and heard a different voice. This woman was patient and explained that all calls out of the country had to be booked twenty-four hours in advance. The outside world, including my family, was sealed off for the next full day.

I felt panicky. I paced the apartment, oppressed now by its dinginess and gloom. I called the international operator again and booked calls for the next day. I cursed the phone system and wondered how I could arrange to be free to cover unexpected news events and also be at home for scheduled international calls necessary to report the events.

After a dinner of Hungarian salami and sweaty cheese I went to bed. I slept well until about 2 a.m. when the doorbell rang. I registered the noise before becoming fully awake. I stumbled from bed, tripped over my suitcase and stubbed my toe on the leg of the desk. Alert now, I walked to the door but did not open it.

"Who's there?"

No one answered.

"Hello, who is it?" I shouted more insistently.

The bell rang again.

"Yaroslav, is that you?"

The bell rang one more time. I opened the door a crack and saw a heavy-set middle-aged man. He had jowls and was unshaven. I suspected the man wanted Yaroslav's cousin and asked him if he would like to leave a message. The man glared at me and said nothing. I wondered if he was drunk. He refused to speak and continued to glower. Eventually I shut the door and went back to bed. The man rang the doorbell until dawn. I woke from what little sleep I had, exhausted and agitated. Each night the man returned and rang the doorbell all night long.

"How do I call the police?" I asked Yaroslav.

"The police, they're probably the ones behind it," he said. "You don't have a registration stamp to be here. Someone wants you out." Tired and completely disoriented, I began to think that I was battling a dark, malevolent force with no face and no name that was bent on driving me from this apartment, possibly from Kiev too.

I began to consider other housing options. Hotels charged foreigners highly inflated rates, so I could not afford a room. I soon also learned that as a foreigner I could not legally rent an apartment. I had nowhere to go. I did not think that anyone would try to hurt me – crime against a foreigner would result in too much unwanted attention in such an insular place as Ukraine. I mustered my dignity and courage and decided to ignore the doorbell ringing. No reaction might end the nightly visits.

Yaroslav gave me a small black cylinder of mace. I slept with the mace on my night table and a pillow over my head to muffle the sound of the doorbell. I still did not sleep well. The doorbell man persisted. My nerves were fraying. I decided I had to find somewhere new to live. Then Yaroslav left for a long holiday. I lost my lifeline.

I told anyone that I met about my housing dilemma. A woman from Rukh felt sorry for me and invited me to stay. We did not know each other well. There was also a large age difference between us. I felt grateful for the offer but also suspicious. I wondered why she had extended the invitation and what she might want from me. I also worried obsessively about language. I had found a Ukrainian teacher but Russian and Ukrainian were so similar that I sometimes confused the two languages. I did not know whether I should speak to her in mangled Ukrainian or more fluent but grammatically incorrect Russian.

On the day of the move, I stood outside my building on Yaroslaviv Val nervously contemplating my move and trying to flag down a car. Forty-five minutes later no one had stopped. This had never happened before.

A man sat in a tan-coloured square Lada across the road. I became convinced that he worked for the KGB and that no motorist would stop while he stayed there. After an hour I became impatient and thought KGB or not, the man could be useful. I asked him for a lift. He said yes and put my bags in the trunk of his car.

I gave the man the correct name of the neighbourhood but the wrong address. I now considered Kiev such an odd and sinister place that I thought it possible the Rukh woman would be punished if the KGB discovered I was her guest.

The man interrogated me along the way.

"Where are you from?"

"Canada."

"Do your parents live there?"

"Yes."

"Are they Canadian Ukrainian?"

"No. My mother is British and my father is Canadian."

"There are no real Canadians. Your father's family must come from this area." I found these questions intrusive but responded to allay the man's suspicion that I was hiding something from him.

"No, he's from a Loyalist family that left Connecticut after the American Revolution. I have no link at all with Ukraine." We approached the outskirts of the city. I found the cracked concrete apartment blocks that lined the road depressing. Most of the balconies looked ready to fall off the buildings. The man began to question me again. He still did not seem to believe that I had no Ukrainian ancestry. Fortunately we arrived at the address I had given the man. I tried to pay. The man refused to take any money.

I dragged my suitcases into the dank entryway of the building where I would not be staying. It smelled of urine. I hid there for an hour. I wondered if I had crossed a line and was no longer thinking rationally. Deep down, I thought not. I peered out to make sure that the man had gone away and would not follow me. I did not see him, so I dragged my suitcases to the correct address.

The entryway of this building smelled of garbage. Otherwise the building looked identical to every other apartment block that stretched across fields as far as I could see. I was marooned beyond the subway line. The building had no elevator, so I trudged up the stairs and knocked on my host's door. She opened it and gave me a welcoming smile that revealed a gold front tooth. Bleak though the surroundings might be, I felt incredibly grateful to have somewhere to stay.

We ate a modest meal and then prepared for bed. I could not understand where I would sleep but did not like to ask. The apartment consisted of one room only, furnished with a two-seat sofa and an armchair. There was no space for anything else. The tiny galley kitchen contained a table, barely big enough to qualify as a table, and two small, square stools. The windowless bathroom had a rough cement floor and a bath faucet that would not stop dripping, no matter how tightly I turned the tap.

When I emerged from the bathroom after brushing my teeth, the former living room had been converted into a bedroom. The sofa and armchair both folded out into beds. Later, when I needed to use the bathroom I had to hopscotch my way across the mattresses to reach the bathroom. I could not possibly inconvenience my host with an extended stay. I would need to find somewhere else to live. Too tired to worry further about accommodation, I fell into a deep, unbroken sleep for the first time since arriving in Kiev.

I was used to roaming where I pleased, but I soon realized the rules differed here. I was a prisoner in Kiev. Once again I thought of Ute and understood her need to escape. I had islands of safety: one, the Rukh office; another, the Foreign Ministry press centre. I remained convinced that Mr. C. and Mr. I. stood as allies in this struggle with that unknown force that wished to deny me accreditation and drive me from every home. I had decided that the large and imposing Mr. I. might kill me if ordered to do so but that he would do it reluctantly, and that for now he was on my side. So, when the press centre asked me to hand in my passport for a registration stamp, I did so willingly, thrilled at the prospect of a stamp that might actually enable me to live somewhere legally. However, when I tried to retrieve my passport, I could not get it back.

4

CHERNOBYL

I saw from the window of Natalia Ivanovna's kitchen how the soft rays of evening August sun turned St. Sophia's gold dome more golden. Hens clucked on the balcony. Natalia Ivanovna and I sipped tea from tin cups. I had met her daughter, Ira, who was a few years older than me, through a colleague. Ira took me in, along with a stray cat named *kotyonok* [kitty]. Natalia Ivanovna allowed us both to stay.

Still passport-less and without accreditation, I dared to hope that my circumstances would soon change. Tomorrow I would make my first trip outside Kiev. A nod and a wink from the Foreign Ministry press centre had enabled me to join a trip to Chernobyl planned by visiting Swiss scientists. I still did not know where I stood with the press centre officials. Sometimes they were strict and scary, but other times they were indulgent and helpful.

"I interviewed one of the liquidators today," I told Natalia Ivanovna.

"Those men were heroes," she said. I thought so too. I told her about Sergei Mertz, a middle-aged engineer who worked at the plant at the time of the accident: "He looked so normal, but when he went to the bathroom his wife listed twelve of his radiation-related illnesses. Sometimes he collapses and has to be rushed to hospital in an ambulance."

Natalia Ivanovna winced. "Poor man," she said. "Most of the firemen died."

They'd been the first responders after operators at the plant carried out a failed experiment that led to fire, an explosion and the release of radioactive material into the air on a scale that surpassed Hiroshima. Even after the firemen had extinguished the blaze, material still smouldered inside the facility that housed the destroyed reactor.

"Mertz said he and his colleagues worried that molten debris might melt through the concrete floor, hit the water table and that the steam build-up would cause another explosion. We call that a China syndrome in English," I said or at least that's what I tried to say. I knew that not all the Russian words I used were that exact. Natalia Ivanovna looked confused. A handsome, thick-waisted no-nonsense woman, she usually told me when I made no sense but tonight said nothing, so I skipped along.

I told her that Mertz and thirteen other volunteers in a team worked around the clock for five days. They tried to enlarge a shaft. They wanted it to accommodate pipes for cooling the reactor.

"They gave us one hundred grams of alcohol for courage before we went in," he said. "The heat was terrible." The volunteers dressed in white lead-lined suits with military air filters.

"It was impossible to breathe in the spaces where we worked," Mertz added. To swelter, suffocate and be irradiated, how much worse could it get? I asked Mertz whether he was forced to help. I could not imagine volunteering for such a job.

"Everyone could refuse and there were instances of people saying, 'I'm afraid, I'm not going in,' but we were the experts and we were the ones who knew the plant, so most of us went in," Mertz explained.

"Heroes," Natalia Ivanovna repeated. She got up and walked slowly toward two burlap bags in the corner of the kitchen. One bulged with potatoes, the other with carrots.

"I grew them myself," Natalia Ivanovna said, her statement full of pride. "They're clean." I learned what clean meant from Ira. I occasionally shopped at the Bessarabskyi Market at the junction of Khreshchatyk and Taras Shevchenko Boulevard. Sometimes lettuce, tomatoes, mushrooms, cucumbers, berries and a whole host of local produce spilled over stalls. Often though, tabletops stood bare, displaying only pickled garlic and jars of pickled tomatoes. On one good day, I came home with a sack of fresh fruit and vegetables. Ira was horrified and made me promise not to shop at the market again.

"Those old *babas* are probably from the Chernobyl region trying to sell you dirty food," she scolded. I had noticed other shoppers asked where food was grown. The names of the regions meant nothing to me, but others must have known which ones were contaminated from the Chernobyl fallout. Ira equipped me with a list of items never to buy. This included nearly all the food that I had purchased.

"Mushrooms and berries are the worst," she insisted. "They suck up radiation." I mentioned this to Yaroslav. He told me that he had a Geiger counter, an instrument to measure radiation levels. "But you have to incinerate the food before you can test it," he said.

Natalia Ivanovna stood at the counter and cleaned her "clean" potatoes. I heard peelings drop into a small bin lined with newspaper.

"Go to bed," she urged. "You have a busy day tomorrow. Have soup for breakfast before you go." She pointed at a pot that already held broth and would soon also be filled with potatoes.

I wished her *"Spokoinoi nochi* [good-night]" and walked out of the kitchen into a dark vestibule, turned right and entered Ira's wing of this large apartment that was really two combined in one. Kotyonok lazed in a corner of Ira's kitchen. Her hamster, which she kept in an aquarium, had saved enough of the bread crusts Ira fed her to make a small ladder. I caught her climbing it, trying to escape. I picked the hamster up, held her for a while, and when I thought she might have forgotten about the ladder, dismantled it. I did not have the heart to take all the bread crusts away and deprive this hamster of her dreams of freedom.

In the morning I walked down the hill to the Dnipro Hotel where the Swiss scientists stayed and boarded their chartered bus for a trip to the "forbidden zone." This thirty-kilometre radius around Chernobyl was no man's land. All the villages had been evacuated and checkpoints surrounded the perimeter to keep everyone out other than those still employed at the Chernobyl plant.

I worried about radiation. In Kiev I studied maps of radioactive fallout. I avoided patches of the city that had been contaminated and also never sat on grass. I dreaded invitations to picnics. Green fields no longer seemed inviting, just potentially toxic.

I discussed radiation safety with the Swiss scientists. They assured me a day trip into the forbidden zone posed no health hazard.

I boarded their bus and sunk into a plush, padded seat. I found a lever to adjust the angle of the back. I tilted the seat as far as it would go in both directions and settled on a position in between. I rested my feet on a conveniently placed metal bar. I swivelled the overhead air vent until the temperature felt just right for me. I had grown accustomed to trips on the trolley-bus, with all the accompanying disadvantages for short people like me. I often stood asphyxiated in the crowds under some taller person's armpit. Deodorant was not widely available, or used, in Kiev.

The chatter on board diminished to a hush as we passed through the checkpoint and barbed wire fence into the zone. Signs stamped Forbidden Zone and No Entry Permitted hung on the fence. Soon after crossing into the zone some scientists asked the bus driver to stop. He opened the door and we all stepped down onto the road. I stayed there as the scientists ventured into nearby fields and forest to collect samples. I heard the clicking sound of Geiger counters all around. Some beeped shrilly at highly radioactive spots.

One scientist returned earlier than the others. He showed me samples of grass and bark that he stored in special plastic bags. He ran his Geiger counter over the specimens. The piercing beeps told me all that I needed to know.

"Follow me," the scientist said.

"Is it safe?"

"Yes, the ground here is perfectly fine. Look," he said as he waved his Geiger counter over the earth. The instrument emitted slow evenly spaced clicks that indicated near normal readings.

"Now listen to this," he said.

He wandered a few paces to the right and waved the Geiger counter again. It let out fast, high pitched beeps. Ground so close by was radioactive even though the patch on which I stood was not.

When all the scientists had returned with their plastic bags filled with flowers, grass, soil, insects, mushrooms and berries, we continued to a nearby village. In such beautiful sunny weather on board a bus full of excited Swiss visitors, I stopped worrying. We drove through the centre of the village to the local administrative building. We all disembarked and climbed the stairs to a reception room.

The organizers invited us to sit at tables draped with white cloths. Several bottles of red wine stood on each. I had not seen wine since an ill-fated video evening. A dozen of those hard-to-come-by bottles had lined my host's hallway that night. We entered the living room. I saw my first video player since arriving in Ukraine and looked forward to a romantic comedy. Although there was scope for error with my patchy Russian, I am certain my host, whom I already suspected worked for the KGB, had not said that we would watch a Swedish porn star perform X-rated acts with a champagne bottle. When he lunged at two of us and held us in a grope and grip that could not be broken, I had visions of blackmail. Headlines flashed through my mind: *Alcoholic, porn-addicted journalist evicted from Ukraine after ménage à trois.* I fought off these memories and focused instead on the local mayor, who now gave a speech.

He explained that his town had been slated for evacuation but that funds had run short, so he and all the residents still lived here. He did not appear to be concerned about radiation, though he ended his speech by telling us that he had chosen to serve red wine instead of vodka because it provided a good antidote to radiation. He urged us to drink as much as we could.

I left before the end of the meal to take a short walk. One block from the building, I met a group of local women.

"A foreigner," one of them shouted.

"How did you know?" I asked.

"Your shoes!" They wore plastic sandals. I had leather loafers. They clustered round me and seemed to speak all at once. I heard:

"They promised to evacuate us. They lied."

"My son doesn't understand radiation. I beg him not to climb trees. I say, 'Ivan, you must never eat apples from those trees.' He always promises but he's mischievous. I find out from others that he and his friends have been in the orchards, eating their fill."

Another woman said, "My mother is the worst. She tells the children, 'I lived through the Second World War. What is this radiation? Where is it? I don't see any. It can't kill you like a bullet or a bomb. Don't listen to your mother, there's no need to worry.'"

I stood there and listened, upset by what I heard. I saw scientists board the bus. I waved goodbye to the women and ran to join the tour. The bus engine was already rumbling. The door slammed shut behind me. The driver took us to Slavutych, about fifty kilometres away from the Chernobyl plant. The town was newly built for Chernobyl evacuees.

Thick forest surrounded Slavutych. The tidy wooden cottages along streets in one neighbourhood reminded me of an alpine resort. After the accident, all the Soviet republics contributed to construction in Slavutych. The Lithuanian government donated the cottages.

I enjoyed being here. The air smelled fresh. Leaves in treetops rustled with the breeze. Dappled light patterned the roads.

I thought of cottage country in Quebéc. This might be a nice place to visit for a holiday.

We met the mayor at the town hall. Armed with statistics for Slavutych, he recited the population figure, the number of housing units, each republic's contribution and the number of construction projects still unfinished. When we asked why so much remained to be done, the mayor said that Soviet authorities had accidentally built Slavutych on land contaminated by radioactive fallout. More than 80 percent of the construction workers fled when they learned the extent of the contamination.

"They told us we were safe here, but now we find we're trapped in a sack," the mayor said. "The population is confined to the town. We can't go out to the forest to gather mushrooms."

I felt the weight of this last statement. Ira had already informed me that mushroom picking, considered a sport in Ukraine, was an important part of weekend family outings. More than once I had been served up dishes of sautéed freshly picked mushrooms and listened to families reminisce about enjoyable days in the woods competing for the best mushroom find. I dreaded eating these mushrooms but always did so to be polite. My mother, a pediatrician, had been the director of a poison control centre in Ottawa. Several species of poisonous mushrooms grew in local woods. She had seen patients with mushroom poisoning from eating some of them. Two of these patients died. My mother had made me promise not to touch any mushrooms that grew wild.

When the mayor finished his talk, we met workers from the Chernobyl plant. They described their daily routine. I was glad not to be alone as I did not know how to respond. What could one possibly say to men and women who dutifully reported to a special "sanitation chamber" near the railway station, where they changed into white cotton outfits before boarding the train bound for Chernobyl. They then transferred to a second train and changed clothes again once they entered the ultra-high-security final ten-kilometre zone surrounding the plant. When work was over, they came home to relax in a radioactive town. I wondered if we were speaking to a group of people who were unwittingly committing suicide.

A Chernobyl host took me to the accident site. I shivered as we stood in front of the destroyed reactor encased in a cement and metal cover, a sarcophagus. I saw no traditional memorial to those who died – no crosses, commemorative plaques, statues or flowers – but this bleak sarcophagus looked like a huge tomb. Cranes and electricity pylons poked up from the landscape. A long patch of desiccated grass ran in front of the reactor. Otherwise I saw only cement, metal, wires and steel. Other reactors nearby still worked. Ghostlike figures dressed all in white scuttled between buildings at the complex. I thought of the men and women that I had met in Slavutych. We did not linger long at Chernobyl.

Our next stop was Pripyat, a modern Soviet city built to house Chernobyl workers, a few kilometres farther down the road. We were going with a Ukrainian MP, Volodymyr Shovkoshytnyi, who had worked at the plant and wanted to visit his old apartment. Although he was middle-aged, he still had the unruly hair of a rebellious student and a long moustache that curved down and made him look sad.

"Come this way," our Chernobyl host said, as he led us into a changing room. "You'll need protective clothing."

"You don't need to change to wear these," he said, pointing to green army fatigues hanging on clothes pegs. The other option was white suits with matching puffy hats that looked like chef's outfits. I chose army fatigues that I could slide over my own clothes and special rubber boots for my feet. Then we boarded a zone mini bus to travel the short distance to Pripyat. "When the bus is too contaminated it will be buried in a graveyard," our Chernobyl host said.

I knew what he meant. A friend who worked in TV had already shown me footage from the time of the accident. Rows and rows of heavily contaminated helicopters, ambulances, buses, cars and trucks, no longer safe to use, filled fields near Chernobyl. Some vehicles were buried but many still lay out in the open. In Kiev, it was difficult to find spare car parts, so they had to be bought on the black market. My mechanic warned me to always go through trusted contacts to avoid contaminated car parts cannibalized from vehicles in the zone.

It only took minutes to reach the checkpoint at Pripyat. The last person that we saw was the guard who waved us in. We drove along a grid of straight streets lined with tall apartment blocks. This city should have been bustling with life, but all we heard was silence. The only noise came from birds that had reclaimed Pripyat. Not a soul came in or out of the deserted apartment blocks. We stared down empty streets. I thought I saw someone standing on a diving board at the local pool. I probably just conjured up a person to try to make this urban ghost town a more normal place. I felt like one of the last survivors on Earth after an apocalypse.

We visited the local fairground. Grass grew as high as the bottom seats of the Ferris wheel. Our Chernobyl host warned us not to step off paved surfaces.

"We wash these down regularly to keep them radiation free," he said. After a brief tour of public sites, Shovkoshytnyi felt ready to face his apartment and all the memories this might trigger. He remembered Pripyat as a lively city. I considered it one huge graveyard and a warning of what might happen in the event of nuclear war.

We walked to Shovkoshytnyi's apartment. We saw dolls propped in windows in many places that we passed.

"They told us we were only being evacuated for a few days," Shovkoshytnyi said. "It happened so fast, we grabbed just a few things. Children left those dolls to welcome us back." When we reached Shovkoshytnyi's building the front door stood ajar.

"Looters have been here," he said. He did not want to touch the door because of radiation contamination. He kicked it with his foot so that it swung open wide. Debris littered the stairwell. Glass crunched underfoot. We climbed slowly, stepping over slippers, badminton rackets, empty picture frames and a home distilling kit.

Shovkoshytnyi's apartment had been spared by the looters. He took the key from his pocket and unlocked the door. We stepped into a time capsule.

"Everything is just as we left it," he said. A frying pan stood on the stove and a flour pot on the counter. Shovkoshytnyi's gym equipment lay on the living room floor. We did not stay long. I could not imagine visiting my past like this. I hoped the trip brought Shovkoshytnyi closure. He sat quietly on the bus during our journey back.

When we arrived at the plant, we took off our protective clothing and boots. Chernobyl workers measured us for radiation. "You're clean," one worker said after he swept me with a Geiger counter. "Take a shower when you get back and make sure you wash your hair." We boarded our own bus. A guard dressed in khaki and open-toed sandals with socks measured radiation levels on the bus tires before waving us on. We drove onto the road and out of the zone.

5

───────────

UKRAINIAN INDEPENDENCE

On a chilly early autumn evening in 1990 I sat on a sofa in the office that Yaroslav and I shared — a studio apartment that Yaroslav "rented" from a friend through some complicated arrangement that let two Ukrainians reach an agreement no foreigner here could. It had been an extraordinary few months. Ukrainians had elected pro-independence Rukh politicians to Parliament. Then the Communists, who dominated Parliament, supported Rukh's declaration of Ukrainian sovereignty. I never thought this would happen so quickly. I felt excited by these political developments but discouraged about my personal circumstances. I wondered who would become independent first — Ukraine or me. I still could not rent an apartment, leave Kiev or do so many things I took for granted in my old life. Working from this office was my one taste of freedom.

It was situated down the hill from Ira's, in the Podil port district. Yaroslav stood in the galley kitchen, stirring a pot of vegetables (clean ones, he insisted) on the stove. He had been away on road trips, reporting from other republics. I envied him this ease of travel. I had been given permission for one visit to Budapest to pick up my car. Otherwise, however, I remained stuck in Kiev, still unable to reclaim my passport. I wished we had a Canadian or British consulate here or someone else who could help. Once in a while I thought of Ute and understood a little better now how she must have felt.

"Want some?" Yaroslav asked as he took the pot off the stove. I nodded yes. He put plates full of ratatouille topped with stringy melted cheese on the table. Then the phone rang. Yaroslav spoke Ukrainian to the caller. When he finished, he turned to me and said "There's going to be a student hunger strike. The students want the Communists out of power. Their demands include the dissolution of Parliament and new elections by spring. We should meet in the square tomorrow morning. They'll set tents up then."

"Wow! This is amazing on top of everything else that's happened. So the students are trying to oust the Communists. Maybe Ukraine will be the new Hungary," I said.

"It's not Hungary here," Yaroslav insisted.

The phone rang again. Yaroslav picked up the receiver and handed it to me. My regular evening call to the foreign desk had come through on time. I pitched the student hunger strike story. Just after my call ended, another one came through. The operator connected Yaroslav to his foreign desk. He worked for a British daily now. He offered the same story as me.

"We're meant to be competitors, not collaborators," I joked after he hung up.

"The rules change when the entire foreign press corps fits in the front seats of a Lada," Yaroslav replied. We finished eating, scrubbed melted cheese from the bottom of the ratatouille pot, washed the rest of the dishes, turned out the light and locked the office for the night. Yaroslav lived with his granny. I drove him home and then went back to Ira's, the wide boulevards free from traffic.

The next morning, I reached October Revolution Square early. I hovered as students equipped with hammers drove tent spikes into the paving stones. I worried that riot police would sweep in and cart the students away on charges of vandalism. The only person who actually appeared was Yaroslav, bleary-eyed, with a knapsack hanging off his shoulder. He wore a black sweatshirt as protection against the morning chill.

"Do you think the police will intervene?" I asked Yaroslav.

"These are students. It wouldn't look good to beat them up," he said. An hour passed. No police officers arrived. A few canvas tents similar to those I had seen in pictures from 1930s camping trips now stood on the square. Students placed plastic sheeting over the tops of the tents to protect them from dew, frost and rain. They camped near a huge red granite Lenin statue, which dominated the square.

"Hi guys," I looked up the steps that led to Lenin and saw our friend Mary, an American Ukrainian lawyer. She volunteered for Rukh.

"I hope they've practised how to handle riot police," she said. Yaroslav, Mary and I milled around as the protesters pitched more tents. By the time we left, a dozen tents stretched down the square. Over the course of the following days, the tent city swelled and support for it grew.

I don't know who was more surprised by the size of the protest when students marched, Mary and me, the police or Communist politicians. That morning I put on Doc Martens, anticipating standing for hours on the streets. I dressed in jeans, a sweater and a large maroon duffle coat. I had my favourite Kiev breakfast, dry cottage cheese–like *tvorog*, topped with *smetana,* a cross between crème fraîche and sour cream. I ate this snow-white mountain from a bowl. Fuelled by black tea, I strolled to the square through streets lined with elegant buildings, enjoying the walk as I always did. I remained in awe of the architecture in central Kiev. No one had described the beauty of this city to me before I arrived. It still amazed me.

As I reached the crest of the hill leading down to Khreshchatyk, I heard a voice amplified through a megaphone. Once I topped the crest and headed down, I had a clear view of the square. It already teemed with students and more were still pouring in along adjacent streets. I joined the throng and watched as organizers took charge.

I spoke to a group of students who said that organizers had barricaded the doors of the library where they studied. The students had gone to the library and had found that the doors were locked. There was a notice about the march on them. They went to the square. Some seemed irritated at the disruption, but most were curious enough to join. A teacher in her late twenties led the last contingent that arrived, a spirited class of twelve-year-olds. The teacher looked as if she was the oldest person in the square.

The organizers shouted instructions through megaphones. Everyone obeyed. First the protesters formed small squads. Then they assembled in orderly lines. Student guards linked arms around the perimeter of the crowd. They walked quickly, to the beat of a drum, toward Parliament. I wondered how MPs would feel when they saw city children on the march.

Mary stood on an embankment near Parliament, a tall, striking figure draped in a heavy, long coat. I climbed the embankment to join her.

"I never thought this many people would turn out," I said.

"It's quite a show," Mary replied. We tried to estimate the size of the crowd (we noticed adults in it now) by counting rows as people marched by. We gave up at 80,000. Still more marchers passed.

The protest worked. The authorities allowed the student leaders a lengthy appearance on TV. The prime minister resigned. The students returned to class, assured concessions on their other demands would follow. They did not. I felt tricked and was sure that the student leaders did too. Momentum dissipated. The atmosphere soon changed in Kiev. Communist leaders organized a large military parade to mark the November 7th anniversary of the Russian Revolution. They banned all protests for that day.

Yaroslav and I both had parliamentary passes that let us cross between city zones established for the parade. We arranged to meet by the Rukh building on the morning of the 7th. We would come from opposite sides of the city.

As I neared the Rukh office, I saw a long military cordon. My pass meant nothing as my path was blocked. I wondered if Yaroslav was faced with a similar situation over on his side. I stared at huge green army trucks. They stood so close together that their wheels nearly touched. Their engines still hummed. The tailpipes spewed diesel fumes. It seemed the trucks might charge forward at any moment.

I stood still, paralyzed by the noise and the size of the trucks. I thought of my accident in London and worried that a truck might move and crush me. I could either inch my way through the crevice to reach the other side so that I could interview trapped Rukh protestors, or I could stay put. I knew that the blockade would not deter Yaroslav. I breathed slowly to calm myself. I smelled diesel, felt vibrations from the engines and fought panic. I rubbed against two walls of black tires as I squeezed through. I reached the other side clammy. My heart raced. I knew that hard-liners had seized charge. All that optimism I had felt for Ukraine just a month ago faded away.

Not long afterwards, the KGB harassed Yaroslav's friend, our office landlady. They interrogated her because she rented the office to Yaroslav and me. She collapsed and ended up in hospital. I felt terrible and was not even allowed to visit her in case my presence made matters worse. In the end we managed to retain the office, but everything seemed so precarious now.

Anxious about the fact that I still had no long-term visa or accreditation papers and that the Foreign Ministry still held my passport, I made an appointment at the Foreign Ministry press office with Mr. I. to discuss my situation. He assured me that I would receive my passport and visa soon and that he hoped accreditation would follow in the New Year.

"I applied for my visa months ago," I half shouted and half pleaded. "I have to get my passport back now." Mr. I. sympathized with my predicament.

"It's with the police *solnyshko*, there's nothing I can do," he said. He claimed not to know which police station held my passport, but I found out. When I showed up, the police officer in charge slammed the door in my face.

Christmas approached. I remained trapped in Kiev. Yaroslav left for New York and would not return. Student protest leaders worried that they might be arrested. Yaroslav did too. He was more vulnerable than me. I understood why he went and was relieved he could leave, though jealous that I could not.

By the time January 1991 arrived, I felt engulfed by gloom. Ira's mother had moved to the dacha. Ira remained in Kiev. I appreciated her company, though I occasionally worried that she might be connected to the KGB. I had long ago reasoned that even if that were true, it didn't matter because I had nothing to hide. Besides she did all the chatting. Language constraints meant that like a family pet, I listened but couldn't really communicate what I thought. I mostly worried, though, that I was a burden. My short-term stay had now dragged on for six months. It could not be easy to have a house guest for so long. One evening mid-month we sat in the kitchen.

"I'm meant to be getting accreditation soon," I told Ira.

"We'll see," she said.

"I'll be able to find a place of my own then," I added. She was kind enough to tell me not to worry about this. We sat for a while longer in her kitchen and drank tea. Then I went to bed. Rukh, as determined as ever to push for Ukrainian independence, was holding a demonstration the next day. I looked forward to it. Activity helped brighten my mood.

A cold wind blew as I made my way toward the demonstration in St. Sophia's Square. I walked quickly and soon saw that people had already gathered there. I noticed a woman who whirled her way through the crowd. So many people knew her. When we passed, she stopped to say hello. Her exuberance won me over on the spot.

"How nice to meet you! I'm Marta," she said and stuck out her hand. Marta had just arrived from New York and would stay for several months. She would establish a bureau for her paper. I had a new friend.

"I was at the Foreign Ministry press office and I think we'll get accreditation soon," she said. "This is important for Ukraine. It's a way to show Moscow that Ukraine has some autonomy."

I did not know what to think. Politics had see-sawed so dramatically throughout the fall and early winter that I could not tell where the power lay – with hard-liners who opposed any move toward independence or with a more moderate faction that seemed to include the Foreign Ministry. I had waited so long for accreditation that I did not even dare to believe that Marta could be right, but a few days later the Foreign Ministry called. Marta and I met Mr. I. and Mr. C. at the press office. Mr. C. smiled when he announced the good news. He handed me my accreditation first.

"Number one for you," he said. Then he handed Marta hers, "Number two for you."

Being number one had never meant so much to me. All those months of anxiety disappeared into the past. I stared down at my laminated card and saw "press" in Cyrillic letters written down the side. I felt free, or as close to it as I could be in Ukraine. Mr. C. congratulated Marta and me. I sensed someone had fought battles behind the scenes to reach this day but doubted I would ever know the details. We chatted a while and then left the office. Marta rushed away to finish a feature. Now that I had official status, I ambled through the neighbourhood and eyed buildings where I would like to live.

A week later I asked Marta, "What if we put apartment wanted ads up in all the buildings that we like?" She laughed and said, "They'll think we're crazy capitalists."

"So? The worst possible outcome is that we'll be ignored." Marta agreed. The next morning I went to her room in the Dnipro Hotel and we drafted ads. Then we drove up to our favourite neighbourhood and posted the ads in the lobbies of the buildings we liked.

Weeks went by with no response. Then a man left a message on my answering machine. Marta and I had already found apartments through her contacts, but I arranged to meet the man anyway. He showed me a large apartment in the centre, diagonally across from where I would live. I thought I would introduce the man to Bill, a British journalist who had visited in the fall and had recently driven back from London to work here. He was staying in a flat owned by Yaroslav's uncle. I walked over and knocked on the door. Bill opened it and peered intently through his wire-rimmed glasses.

"How was the trip back?" I asked. Bill held a thick book in one hand and a bar of deodorant in the other.

"I stocked up on petrol in Poland," he explained. "I filled tins in the back but didn't shut the lid properly on one. Petrol sloshed all over a box of books." I watched as he rubbed deodorant over a page of his book and then flipped it and rubbed more on the next one.

"Best thing to counteract the smell," Bill said. I saw boxes full of tinned food in the hallway. Bill invited me nearly every night afterwards for dinner and always let me choose a tin to open. When the food ran out, we ate porridge and persimmons, the only fruit available in the Bessarabskyi Market. Occasionally we found an Azeri pomegranate.

I began to dream about food. I called an American friend in Moscow. I had visited hard-currency grocery stores there and remembered rows of fresh produce.

"I'm dying for an orange," I told him. "I've actually started to dream about salmon and snow peas. I wonder if that means I'm malnourished. All you can get here is pickled garlic, shredded pickled carrots and pickled tomatoes."

I asked my friend whether he would shop for a small group in Kiev and send the food down by train. He agreed and wise to Russian ways, bribed the female wagon attendant in one car. She kept the groceries in her cabin. Everything was there when I collected the shipment.

I finally felt settled in Kiev. Even work went well. In Hungary I had chased news. Here, at least until now, little competition meant that I only had to sit still and news arrived. It came through visits from strangers, phone calls, envelopes stuffed full of documents surreptitiously shoved under a door, or from some opposition members during a walk in the park, where they escaped bugs (the electronic kind). Even the chairman of Parliament, Leonid Kravchuk, left his office door open. Ukrainian journalists wandered in, so I did as well, though that door soon closed. With a formal foreign press corps, the rules changed.

Now we sat together in a press gallery that overlooked the chamber of Parliament. A white Lenin statue stood in a nook behind the high table where Mr. Kravchuk and his associates sat. That winter Marta, Bill and I followed manoeuvring between Moscow and Kiev over a referendum planned for March. The referendum, if passed, would confirm the continued existence of the Soviet Union but would decentralize some powers to the republics like Ukraine.

By the time the vote occurred in March, western Ukraine and the Chernobyl region had added a question on Ukrainian independence to the ballot. Both those regions voted in favour of independence. The result did not constitute an immediate challenge as the majority voted in favour of the union, but it was something to note.

Another foreign journalist arrived. She came from Oxford to do research for her PhD but set that aside to temporarily report for a British paper. This second Marta in our press corps was from Toronto. Now we had Bill, New York Marta, Toronto Marta and me. We nearly occupied a full row in the parliamentary press gallery.

I watched, fascinated by this game of cat and mouse, as the Ukrainian Parliament pushed for more control over areas previously under Moscow's authority. Parliament in Kiev created a new position of president of the Republic and explored ways it might be able to control deployment of Ukrainian troops in the Soviet army. I wondered, along with so many others, how Moscow would respond.

Negotiations were under way for a new Union Treaty between Moscow and the republics. It seemed that some of Ukraine's initiatives might be endorsed. Leonid Kravchuk spoke of sovereignty for Ukraine in nearly every speech but still embraced the Union. I could never tell where his emphasis lay. He was skilled in saying two different things at once, which sometimes left me understanding nothing at all. Then, in early August 1991, President Bush arrived in Kiev.

Summer holidays meant that few journalists remained in Kiev. New York Marta had gone home. Her replacement, Lesyia, had arrived.

"What a disappointment!" Toronto Marta said as we sat together in the press gallery after Bush spoke. Journalists quickly dubbed this Bush's Chicken Kiev speech. Phrases that I jotted down included "suicidal nationalism" and "the suicidal course of isolation." Bush wanted Ukraine to stop asserting sovereignty so that Washington could maintain the status quo in relations with Moscow.

I saw Lesyia enter the press gallery. She waved and joined us, discussed the speech, then got up to leave.

"Are you going to Chervona Ruta?" Marta asked Lesyia.

"When is it again?"

"In two weeks," Marta said. "You guys should come. All the best bands are playing." I had not heard of Chervona Ruta, so I asked for the details.

"It's an alternative music festival that started two years ago in western Ukraine. This year the festival will be in Zaporozhye in southern Ukraine, a Russified region. The festival is partly cultural and partly political. The bands are great and very Ukrainian. The idea is to expose people in a Russified region to Ukrainian culture and music and to make them aware of Ukrainian identity. A lot of the musicians sing in Ukrainian, not Russian," she explained.

"Is this Ukraine's Woodstock?" I asked.

"Sort of," said Marta. "Chervona Ruta is the name of a love song written by Volodymyr Ivasiuk in the late 1960s. His song became a hit, but he was hassled by the KGB because the song was very Ukrainian at a time when all things Ukrainian were repressed. In the early 1970s Ivasiuk died. The authorities said he committed suicide by hanging himself from a tree. Everyone thought the KGB killed him."

"How awful," I said, sickened by the image. "It's nice that organizers named the festival in his honour. I'd love to go, if you don't mind company."

"Great," Marta said.

"I might also bring a guest. I'm not sure when he'll arrive, but it should be some time soon."

"Do tell!" Marta said.

"There's not much to say. I only know that he's another British journalist named Stephen. A friend of mine is meant to host him. Since I have a spare room, he asked if Stephen could stay with me until Stephen finds his own place."

"The more the merrier," Marta said. Lesyia said she'd go as well.

* * *

Marta and I shared a room in the Zaporozhye hotel. We compared notes on bands we had heard. I loved the ones that wove folk into rock. They created such a unique sound.

"I met Andriy Sereda," I told Marta. I said how surprised I was to bump into this famous musician, standing barefoot, in a stadium corridor. "He described this festival as the musical rebirth of Ukraine."

"He's right," Marta said.

"He thinks that even if people don't understand politics that they'll intuitively realize the Union Treaty is harmful for Ukraine," I told her.

The treaty was due to be signed soon, but we didn't really feel like talking about politics. It was just fun to be here listening to music. I sat on my bed. Marta brushed her long, thick hair. A crystal pendant hung from her neck. Pretty and slender, Marta was on her way out.

"Don't wait up for me!" she said. She laced up her Doc Martens.

"I know, I'm a bedtime wimp," I told her. Marta, a night owl, would party for hours more. Our body clocks did not match.

A few minutes after she left, I went to join Stephen and Lesyia for a drink downstairs.

As I walked down the corridor, I saw the lady who monitored our hallway (many Soviet hotels had them) planted in a chair behind her desk. Her body spilled over the frame.

"Girl, leave your key with me," she commanded. I pointed out that I would still be in the hotel, just downstairs, but handed the key over to appease her.

I took the elevator down to the bar. Lesyia and Stephen sat at a table. A tinny version of a popular song played on the sound system. I slid into a spare seat at the table.

Stephen, still reeling from culture shock, peered through his glasses across the bar, observant of details that I no longer noticed.

"Is that a lady of the night?" he asked. Lesyia and I shifted in our seats and saw a tall, slim young woman with the type of blonde hair that came from a bottle and a skirt so short that it might be confused with underwear.

"Could be," Lesyia said.

"Bill knows someone who wanted to be a hard-currency prostitute," I told them. "Apparently lots of her friends at university did too."

"Oh come on," Lesyia said.

"That's what she said."

"Do you want us to leave you alone so you can find out?" Lesyia asked Stephen. We heard a ripple of laughter from Stephen, "Not particularly," he said. We chatted a while longer. Midnight struck. August 18th slipped into August 19th. I felt ready for bed.

I woke early in the morning. Marta was still asleep. I dressed quietly and left the room. I went down to the restaurant for breakfast. I saw no one that I knew, so I ate quickly, alone. Sombre classical music played on the sound system in the restaurant. It seemed an odd choice for a hotel filled with rock festival guests. I gobbled down two undercooked eggs on untoasted bread, sipped black tea and then returned to the room. I opened the door quietly as Marta usually did not rise until shortly before noon. I tiptoed in, rounded the corner and, to my surprise, found her wide awake and fully dressed.

"There's been a coup in Moscow," she said. She seemed to be in shock, as was I.

We rushed out of the room to find friends and more information. No one knew much. A brief recording periodically interrupted classical music. It still streamed dirge-like from all radios. The announcement said that a committee of hardline Communist leaders (the GKChP) now ruled in Moscow. I knew that these hard-liners had opposed the Union Treaty, afraid the general secretary of the Soviet Communist Party, Mikhail Gorbachev, would give too much power away to the republics. Gorbachev, who was on holiday in his dacha in Crimea, a Black Sea peninsula just a little farther south than us, was under house arrest. I felt shocked to imagine him there, in a place that should be a relaxing sea-side retreat, but was now a jail.

We spoke briefly with the head of Rukh, Viacheslav Chornovil. This brave man had been imprisoned in labour camps until the mid-1980s for speaking out against Communism. He joked now that coup leaders might send him back to the Gulag. I worried that joke might come true.

Marta and I found Lesyia and Stephen. We looked for fast Kiev-bound transport. We found a taxi driver who would make the day-long trip. We started out calmly enough. I held my shortwave radio out the window to capture the best possible reception for BBC news bulletins. The taxi driver wanted updates, so we translated the news for him, which was probably not a good idea. One journalist reported that tanks and troops were headed toward Kiev. The taxi driver seemed to channel all his anxiety through the accelerator pedal. We careened for several hours along a violently potholed "highway" from Zaporozhye back toward Kiev. No one wanted to sit in the front seat with its frighteningly panoramic view of all the things we might hit.

We saw one tank camouflaged on the outskirts of Kiev as we drove in. However, by the time we reached the centre, the city looked completely normal. The scent of freshly baked bread wafted through our taxi as we passed a local bakery. Customers lined up at a busy café nearby.

We had been in touch with Mary, who had stayed in Kiev. We found her and asked how Kravchuk had responded to events in Moscow. She gave us a concise lawyerly update: "Kravchuk hasn't come out for or against the coup. He's sitting on the fence. I've seen the coup leaders on TV. They look drunk. I think they're scared."

All the drama occurred in Moscow. Boris Yeltsin, president of the Russian Federation, denounced the coup. Tanks appeared in the streets. One battalion switched sides and backed Yeltsin. He climbed on a tank to rally his supporters, who braced for an attack from the hard-liners. Nothing like this happened in Kiev. I drifted through the halls of the Writer's Union, around the corner from Parliament, where Rukh held some of its press conferences. I searched for news but found none. Everyone here waited, just like me.

I left the building and walked down the hill to my apartment on Karl Marx Street. I opened the door to stillness and accumulated dust. A light on the answering machine by the phone flashed. When I played the messages, I heard one from the Canadian embassy that recommended evacuation from Kiev. I erased it.

We still waited for someone to take a decision, for Kravchuk to rebel or for coup leaders to introduce marshal law in Ukraine, but nothing happened. When it was clear that the coup had failed, Kravchuk called a press conference for foreign journalists. He described a visit from the commander of Soviet Ground Forces, General Valentin Varennikov and a group of other Soviet generals who had marched into his office. The general told him to remove a portrait of Gorbachev from the wall, and ordered Kravchuk to support the coup.

"I did everything that I could to prevent tanks from crushing people," Kravchuk said. He smouldered. I sensed a change in Kravchuk, a new anger at this personal violation by Moscow military men who threatened him. But Rukh leaders appeared furious with Kravchuk because he took so long to denounce the coup. Some reform-minded Communists and military leaders in Ukraine had spoken out against it before Kravchuk. I talked with friends. We heard rumours of a new push for independence, dissected tensions between Rukh and the Communists and wondered what would happen at an emergency session of Parliament that would be held soon.

On August 24th, I awoke to sun that streamed in my front windows and a burble of noise from nearby. I lived alone in an apartment on the top of an elegant six-floor turn-of-the-century building, just around the corner from Khreshchatyk. My balcony backed onto October Revolution Square.

My landlord's father had planted the palm tree that now soared nearly twelve feet over the bed. He carved extra rooms from space deemed unlivable by Stalin-era inspectors, who enforced strict space allocations; he covertly turned a nook above the staircase landing into a study. He also wrapped a garbage chute pipe that jutted from the wall in plastic, covered it with a polished five-sided mahogany wood box and placed a plant holder on top. A service corridor became his dining room.

The noise surprised me. I never heard street sounds way up here in my private retreat. I lay still and stared up at the palm leaves, wanting to investigate but still comfortable in bed. A few minutes later, I wiped the sleep from my eyes and got up. A moth fluttered past. I had previously located the cupboard where some nested in a pile of my landlord's old clothes. I cleaned the clothes and thought I had dealt with the moths. The odd one that I continued to see soon exploded into a cloud of sweater-eating menaces. I stuffed every cupboard full of moth balls and invested in expensive pheromone traps. However, they still multiplied and my wardrobe began to disintegrate.

Wide awake now, I chased the moth and caught it, no easy task in a place covered in patterned wallpaper that offered good camouflage. I continued down the corridor past the galley kitchen, through the dining room and out French doors onto the balcony. I peered through leaves on branches that swayed right next to my balcony and caught glimpses of a crowd gathered in October Revolution Square. Usually piano melodies floated skywards as students at the conservatory across the courtyard practised. That morning I heard the sound of megaphones and chants.

I made coffee and toast, washed, changed and went out to investigate. On Khreshchatyk, a car passenger shouted through a megaphone, "Don't be a sheep, march with us to Parliament." A sea of blue and yellow Ukrainian flags fluttered over the square. It was happening. Rukh had drafted a declaration of independence for Ukraine. Today it would be put to a vote in Parliament. I felt excited but guarded. I could not believe that Rukh would win.

A group of us monitored the debate from the press gallery in Parliament. During a break, I left Parliament with another journalist to gather comments from people on the streets. The journalist wore a tie; I put on my suit jacket. When we stepped out the door, we saw that the crowd gathered in October Revolution Square had now massed outside Parliament.

"*Han'ba*! [Shame]." I heard someone shout. More jeers and chants followed. I looked behind; no one stood there. I soon realized these jeers were hurled at us, which came as a shock. People mistook us for Communists who were trying to leave. I knew the crowd would prevent this in order to preserve Parliament's required quorum for an independence vote. So this is how a Communist in Rukh territory would be – exposed, outnumbered, fearful of what could happen next. Mostly, though, I felt indignant to be mistaken for one.

I saw Sashko, The megaphone man. He shouted, *"nashyi* [ours]." Those words meant rescue. The jeers died down. People swarmed us for a different reason now. Although they could hear the official proceedings broadcast over speakers outside Parliament, they wanted news of behind-the-scenes manoeuvrings inside. We told them what we knew and learned that they would block all the doors to Parliament until the vote passed. The journalist and I separated. I returned to the press gallery. Parliament soon recessed.

"The Commies are going downstairs to figure out how they should vote," Lesyia said.

"I can't imagine them opting for independence, though Kravchuk seems a changed man since the coup," I remarked. We discussed how hardline Communists in Ukraine might respond.

We parted ways, doubting whether Rukh would win enough support for independence.

I milled about in the hallway, held my shortwave radio and moved from window to window until I found a spot for good radio reception. The BBC news bulletin began with an announcement that Communist Party activities in Moscow had just been suspended. I could not believe what I heard. The Communist Party held the Soviet Union together. It was impossible to imagine the Soviet Union could survive without it. I shouted to friends in the hallway. They crowded around to listen to the broadcast. English speakers translated the news for Ukrainians.

When the broadcast ended, people drifted away. I tried to absorb the implications of what we had just heard. I went back to the press gallery. Soon MPs returned. The Rukh independence motion was read out for a vote. A friend translated the motion as follows: "As of 24 August, 1991, Ukraine is an independent democratic state. Only the constitution of Ukraine and its government's resolutions are valid on Ukrainian territory."

I sat on the edge of my seat as MPs below pressed their buttons for the vote. I had moved to Kiev and stayed through those early difficult months, hoping for this very moment.

An electronic board displayed the tally – only two MPs voted against independence. We leaped out of our seats in the press gallery and leaned far over the railing to watch MPs below. Bursting with excitement, we speculated about what would happen next; mostly, though, we took a minute to savour the moment. We had just witnessed history. I wanted to gauge the reaction outside, so I ran out into the lobby and peered down from a window at the square. A huge crowd stood by the main door to Parliament. People held a Ukrainian flag the size of a football field stretched out between them. Then the door to Parliament opened. A small group of MPs marched the flag into the chamber.

The next morning my mind still raced to understand what had tipped the balance in Rukh's favour and made hardline Communists vote for independence. I thought maybe they felt cast adrift when Moscow suspended Communist Party activities and that a vote for Ukrainian independence was a vote for the survival of the Ukrainian Communist Party. I went for a morning walk up the hill, toward the Communist Party headquarters. A small group of people stood outside.

"They're about to seal the doors," a stranger told me. "City Council has already cut off communications inside."

"But the Communist Party still legally exists here," I said, confused.

"The building stands on city land, so the council says it's authorized to seal it," the stranger explained. I stood with the crowd, curious to see what would happen next. A few men walked up the steps of this massive white columned building into the lobby. More followed. I trailed behind. We climbed the central staircase. Small groups had already entered a main office. When I arrived, papers lay strewn across the floor. One man riffled through a filing cabinet. Another one shoved Communist Party letterhead in his pockets.

Then someone shouted "I found it!"

I turned and saw a man who waved a pad of ink. He also held a Communist Party stamp. I understood his excitement. I had waited so many months for visas and accreditation with that type of official stamp that I almost wanted to grab the stamp from him and hold onto power for a while. I realized, though, that what was worth so much a day ago was worthless now.

Stamps and paper aside, the looters took nothing of value. Soon they left as a group, walked down the stairs and lined up to polish their shoes on a machine by the door. When everyone had left the building, City Council members sealed the big wooden doors with offically stamped paper. Soon prominent figures, including Leonid Kravchuk, announced their resignations from the Communist Party. Kravchuk said that he had actually quit the party on the first day of the coup.

So many people wanted to know what was happening in Ukraine. All of us filed stories daily and became almost nonchalant about those once-coveted bylines. With such rapid change, it was hard to decide which stories to cover and where to go. Ukraine had pledged to become non-nuclear in its declaration of sovereignty, but the Americans, in particular, worried about what would happen to nuclear weapons on Ukrainian territory. Russia threatened revision of its border with Ukraine if Ukraine seceded from the union. I flew down to Crimea, where I investigated rumours that Crimea might break away from Ukraine and join Russia. Ukraine began to build an army and refused to remit hard-currency funds to Moscow.

Then one day in early November Bill called.

"You know how the Chechens joined up with the Ingush, declared independence and voted General Dzhokhar Dudayev as their president last month?" he said. With all that had been happening in Ukraine, I hadn't paid much attention to events in Russia's Caucasus region.

"What! Russia's unravelling?" I shouted.

"Yeltsin's declared a state of emergency and is flying troops down to restore order. I'm going to Grozny to cover it. I've got to run."

After we hung up, I sat in my kitchen and thought about what Bill told me. Chechnya was in Russia, so I had no claim on the story, but I wanted to go anyway. I called the foreign editor and got permission. After our conversation, I felt queasy, almost weak in the knees, and wondered if I should cancel. I phoned Stephen instead. He was also planning a trip to Chechnya. We decided to travel together.

6

CHECHNYA

"Do you have a will?" I asked Stephen. "No," he said. "Perhaps it's time to write one." We sat on hard chairs in the departure lounge at Boryspil airport, the air clouded with cigarette smoke, waiting for our flight to board and our journey to Chechnya to begin.

I felt discouraged by Stephen's answer. I thought he might just make a joke and dismiss my question, but if someone so rational considered a will necessary then he must also think death a possibility. I rummaged in my knapsack for a pen and paper and wrote out my will, though I wondered if it would be legally valid. I had a mother, father, brother and sister, few possessions and only a little money. I divided everything that I had, tucked the will away in a money belt with my passports, recapped my pen and then searched the departure lounge for food. I did not want to think about death any longer.

Our flight left on time. The plane climbed steeply. The temperature in the cabin dropped. I wore my winter coat and now reached inside the pockets for gloves that I put on. I dozed fitfully as our jet lurched through the air. We received no comfort or an explanatory announcement from crew members when the plane dropped suddenly. Heads banged and a dog barked. I heard the clang of buckles as people strapped themselves into their seats, not all successfully. One man, whose seat belt had become unattached trapped a stewardess in the aisle. He waved the seat belt that should have been attached to his seat and demanded that it be secured there again.

We faced a long trip. The airport in Grozny was closed, so we flew to Mineralnyie Vodi, a Russian city still a long drive from Grozny. When we landed, we found a taxi and began our journey south through the Caucasus mountain range – Nazran first, the capital of Ingushetia (a Chechen ally), and then Grozny. With so many hours stretching ahead in the taxi, I forgot about our destination and slipped into a zone of timelessness. I watched scenery unfold through the windows. We meandered across dusty foothills, mountain valleys and up steep roads, through passes with views of craggy snow-capped mountains.

"Mount Elbrus is the tallest," Stephen said, "about 5,600 metres." I could not process such a figure but felt contained securely behind rock walls. Conflict nearby seemed unimaginable; these bucolic valleys radiated peace, not bloodshed and strife. We stopped at a hotel for the night. The next morning we woke to see the mountain peaks lit with the soft glow of early day sun.

After breakfast, we continued our journey by taxi. Soon the landscape changed again. Near Nazran we arrived at a makeshift road block and a mass of men. No one wore a uniform or had a gun, at least not one that was visible. The checkpoint consisted of rocks heaped in a large mound and a metal bar across part of the road. About a hundred men and boys stood on or near this barricade. They formed an additional human barrier that prevented passage. Cars pulled up alongside the road. The only visible women sat as occasional passengers in these cars.

Our taxi driver stopped. Stephen and I got out of the car and approached the barricade. I smelled the rank scent of oily smoke; black plumes rose from fires that burned in the centre of old tires. Sombre men — their mouths straight slashes, no smiles here — stood at the barricade. They all wore fedoras or square fur hats. Some dark-haired boys, hatless and in sweaters, shouted and waved sticks in the air. Others ran along ditches. They watched as more cars reached the barricade and stopped. The crowd of stuck travellers swelled.

We could not tell who controlled this roadblock. Men and boys seemingly drifted here from places nearby. No one appeared to hold an official position.

"Good afternoon," Stephen said as he approached one large, middle-aged man. "We're foreign journalists."

"Where are you from?" the man asked.

"Britain," Stephen replied. Suspicious, the man asked Stephen more questions. When we showed him our accreditation cards, he relaxed and shouted "foreign journalists."

A younger man, small and with a bushy moustache, stepped out from the crowd. He told us that he lived in Grozny: "I can take you there," he said. We paid our taxi driver and collected our bags.

I felt nervous as I slammed the trunk of the taxi shut. This was the point of no return. The driver started his engine and disappeared in a cloud of dust. The men raised the barrier. Stephen and I passed through and set foot in what these men called the independent Chechen-Ingush Republic; however, Russians still called it part of Russia. I could not imagine Russia would allow Chechnya to just slip away quietly. Bill and Stephen had already worked in conflict zones. I had not. I realized that maybe I only visited one now because I felt competitive with my friends. I caught up with Stephen, who was already standing by the car. When I reached it, our new driver introduced himself.

"Vakha," he said. A smile broke out from under his moustache.

Stephen and I asked Vakha whether the barricade had been there for long.

"Already for several days."

"Have Russian troops arrived?" I asked and hoped that my voice betrayed none of the anxiety that I felt. Stephen seemed so calm.

"Yes," he said. "But we trapped them at the airport. They're leaving." When we asked for details, Vakha told us that Russian troops had landed in Grozny. Chechen fighters immediately surrounded the planes and refused to let any soldiers out. I felt quite worried by this development. I could not imagine that the Russian military would tolerate such humiliation for long and wondered about conditions the soldiers had endured on board. I imagined an interior clouded with smoke, bored, stressed soldiers who puffed on cigarettes, the smell of in-demand toilets, guns and ammunition everywhere and wondered whether the Chechens had given the soldiers any food or water.

"We will defeat the enemy," Vakha said as an almost casual afterthought. We got into the car and headed for Grozny. After travelling for some time, we stopped by a small house on a residential street in the suburbs.

"Is the hotel nearby?" I asked.

"We'll eat now," Vakha said. "Then I'll take you to the hotel." He led us to the back door of the house. He took Stephen through to the living room. When Stephen had passed, two women appeared at the kitchen door. Their heads were covered in brightly patterned scarves. They smiled and said hello. They introduced themselves as our host's wife and daughter. They wanted to talk (I did too), but Vakha reappeared and insisted that I join Stephen in the front room. I did not know whether to feel pleased that he treated me as an honorary man and let me sit there or offended that he rushed me away, as if I might somehow corrupt his wife and daughter.

Stephen and I sat on a sofa while Vakha walked back and forth between the kitchen door and the living room. His wife and daughter handed him various objects for the table, which he carried back – knives and forks, glasses, plates and then finally steaming bowls of meat.

Then Vakha arranged chairs at the table and invited Stephen and me to eat. He remained standing by the table. I felt uncomfortable with this arrangement, a burden on our host. Stephen asked, "Won't you join us?"

Vakha explained that as the youngest brother in a Muslim family, his male siblings cared for him and in exchange he served them. He waited on his elder brothers when they visited as he did with us now. Nothing we said could persuade Vakha to sit with us for long at the table. Once or twice he briefly did but then sprang to his feet again.

With Vakha shuttling back and forth to the kitchen, Stephen and I had time to look at our surroundings and could not help but notice a large gun that hung on the wall. When Vakha returned after one kitchen trip, Stephen glanced at the gun and asked, "Does it work?"

"Of course," Vakha replied. "A house is not a Chechen house without a gun." On the wall the gun looked harmless, a quaint relic of days gone by. We chatted about local politics and then later, about more personal matters, a topic that I had learned to dread.

"Are you married?" Vakha asked me.

"No, I'm afraid not."

"How old are you?" I mumbled that I was in my twenties. "And still not married? Find her a husband," he ordered Stephen. I asked Vakha how he and his wife met.

"I kidnapped her." I wasn't sure that I understood, so I checked with Stephen, who confirmed that is what Vahka had said.

"Why did you kidnap your wife?" Stephen asked.

"It's our custom. When a man sees a woman that he likes, he and his friends will kidnap her. If her family does not free her, then she's his to keep." I felt so shocked by this custom that I did not know what to say. I understood a little better now why Vakha kept his daughter locked in the kitchen but wondered how she felt about the arrangement. I guessed she was about seventeen. By that age I had already travelled through Europe alone. I did not think my freedom would be impinged upon here. Already an old maid by local standards, who would want to kidnap me?

Stephen and Vakha chatted more. I wanted to talk to the women in the kitchen but stayed put. Eventually Stephen and I smiled and tapped our watches – time for hotel check-in.

"I'll drive you there," Vakha said. I appreciated his hospitality but felt a bit ashamed as well. I doubted such kindness would be reciprocated at home. Who would pick up two strangers there, chauffer them between cities and then take them home for an impromptu meal? I wondered if Vakha's wife and daughter kept extra supplies in the fridge, or whether we had just eaten food that was supposed to have been their dinner. The women remained cloistered in the kitchen. We could not thank them directly; we asked Vakha to do so on our behalf.

As we approached the city centre, we saw men on the streets with guns. The first armed man that I spotted wore high-topped soft leather boots with his trouser bottoms tucked inside. A black leather jacket similar to Stephen's hung loosely over his torso; a tall astrakhan hat sat tower-like on his head. He slung a rifle over his shoulder. He ambled down the street with his gun through a crowd of women who carried bags of shopping home, clusters of small children, and the occasional straight-backed man in military dress. As we entered the streets adjacent to the central square, the number of men with guns increased and the city acquired the look of one on the brink of conflict. Déjà vu strikes at the most unexpected moment.

I thought suddenly of one memorable childhood Halloween. I recalled that strange atmosphere of military might in our quiet residential Ottawa neighbourhood, which seemed devoid of threat and need for protection. The politics at home also constituted a fight over independence. French Canadian separatists in the province of Québec wanted to break away from Canada. Too young to understand politics, I just felt excited to receive candy from soldiers with guns who guarded houses on our Halloween route. A tank was parked in a field by our school. Soldiers in fatigues camped in the garden at one friend's house because her father was a cabinet minister. Sometimes they smiled, but they always refused to play with us. We thought of this military presence as one big, exciting game. I did not fully understand the concept of death but remembered a joke told in the school-yard about the murder that triggered the War Measures Act and the presence of all the soldiers who guarded government officials and diplomats. Separatists had kidnapped James Cross, a British diplomat, and Pierre Laporte, a Québécois politician. They killed Pierre Laporte but released James Cross.

"Why did Cross survive?

"Because he stood behind Laporte [the door]."

Even then I knew that joke should not be told.

Mostly, though, we played as close to all the military hard-ware as we were allowed to. We had no weapons but imitated the soldiers. We turned sticks into rifles. Here in Grozny some did the same. Men without guns armed themselves with planks of wood and canisters of gasoline. They helped blockade the entrance of one government building.

Our car turned into a side street. Vakha stopped. He pointed down the road. "Your hotel is just a little farther along," he said. We thanked Vakha for his help and said goodbye. As we approached, we saw that a pair of unmanned machine guns mounted on tripods with bullet magazines hanging down from them flanked the hotel entrance.

I wished Vakha had invited us to stay the night. This place seemed braced for siege with the possibility of conflict now alarmingly real. As we entered the lobby, I wondered about this hotel, where loaded guns just stood around. I looked for soldiers who might own them but saw only the usual staff — a surly receptionist at the front desk, waiters who scurried past on their way to the restaurant. Were the waiters also combat soldiers? Would they man the machine guns if Russians attacked? I stifled my sense of dread. Stephen took the machine guns in stride; so would I.

We checked in. The telephone in our room worked, which was a huge relief. Sporadic gunfire echoed through the streets.

I slipped away to the reception desk and asked questions in private. I wanted assurance that no Russians were approaching Grozny. The receptionist, softened now, seemed ready to chat. I asked her about the gunfire.

"Don't worry, it's a celebration," she said.

"Are you sure that's not fighting?" I asked.

"No, there's no one to fight, at least not yet."

"So the Russian soldiers have withdrawn?" She nodded yes. Stephen and I had heard this as well and had actually seen some of the buses full of disarmed Russian soldiers leaving, but the state of emergency declared by Yelstin remained in effect and no one knew what would happen next.

"There are so many people out there with guns. Do you think there could still be conflict?" The receptionist shrugged her shoulders. She didn't know.

I needed better information. I decided I would cross the square. Someone at the government buildings on the other side must know the current state of affairs.

I walked out the lobby, past the machine guns and stepped into the street. I could still hear the pop of occasional gunfire but saw no sign of fighting. My father had trained as a pilot during the Second World War. Even though he disliked violence, including hunting, he taught my brother, my sister and me how to shoot his rifle and pistol when we were children. He also taught us respect for weapons. He told us that bullets from guns fired in the air still kill when they fall back to land. In Grozny no one gave this much thought. I did not want to be anywhere nearby when a celebratory bullet came down.

I crossed the central square. It teemed with armed and unarmed people. A row of about twenty men kneeled on one strip of grass. It was desiccated and yellow, almost a carpet of straw. The men had spread their prayer mats on top and placed their boots in front of the mats, alongside their guns. They covered their heads, placed their hands on their thighs and prayed facing east. A pale blue sky stretched wide overhead. I had not heard a call to prayer, but perhaps I had just missed it. Such public prayer in Grozny must be a new development. Religion had been so furtive under Communism.

I reached government buildings on the far side of the square. Men stood in a line; most of them wore astrakhan hats. They blocked the main entrances. One held a green flag with a star and crescent. There was no sign of the Russian colours here. The men directed me to the information office upstairs. They parted and allowed me into the building.

I climbed the stairs and knocked on the information office door.

"Enter," I heard a woman say. I opened the door and cheered up immediately. This could be any secretary's office with two-tone walls, sparse furnishings and an enormous blue typewriter that spanned the width of the desk. This secretary, if that's what she was, glowed with warmth and excitement. Part of that glow came from carefully applied rouge, lipstick and eyeliner, but most of it came from within. The only splash of colour in her outfit came from her bright headscarf. Otherwise she was all dressed in black. A fringe of light brown hair peeked out from under her scarf. What I noticed most was the Kalashnikov rifle that she cradled in her arms, the green canvas strap slung over her shoulder. I stood there fascinated by this secretary warrior.

"Susan," I said by way of introduction. "I work for a British paper. May I ask you some questions?" She said that I could.

"Aren't you afraid? Are you really ready to fight the Russians?" She said she was and that most people expected more Russian troops to arrive since Yeltsin's declaration of emergency was still in place. But she also said that Russian leaders hadn't sanctioned the use of force. Relieved to hear that last point, I made my second request. I wanted to interview the man in charge of the Chechen-Ingush Republic, General

Dzhokar Dudayev. She gave me his number. Business over, our conversation drifted elsewhere.

"Is that your gun?" I asked.

"I borrowed it."

"Are you a soldier?"

"No, but I know how to fight." I told the secretary that my father had taught me to shoot but that I felt uncomfortable around guns.

"We're used to them here. In school, we learned how to assemble a Kalashnikov from parts. Then we had to run up a hill and fire into sand," she said. I told her that in our non-academic school courses we learned how to do handstands and bake macaroni and cheese. I did not stay long. As I left the secretary's office, she shouted after me "Are you interviewing the hijackers?"

I returned and received contact details for one of the men who had recently hijacked an Aeroflot flight from Mineralnye Vody to Turkey. The hijackers had threatened to blow up the plane and all the passengers on board if Russia did not pull its troops back from Chechnya. The hijackers were back home in Grozny now. All the passengers had been set free.

The next day passed fairly uneventfully. Yeltsin's declaration of emergency remained in force. Stephen and I wandered the streets. Men in the square brewed tea on the eternal flame. Officials in government offices still waited with their guns, ready to defend the Chechen-Ingush Republic. A man brandishing a sword burst into our hotel room. He said a Russian spy had been arrested and wanted us to interview him.

The following morning I felt uneasy when I saw a Jeep filled with leather-clad men pull up in front of the hotel. They had come to pick me up for my interview with General Dudayev. I climbed on board. We careened around corners, raced down roads and pulled up in front of the building where General Dudayev worked. We entered the building and passed a contingent of guards in the lobby. We walked down a hallway lined with machine guns on stands and finally reached a door. One of the security men knocked and then opened the door. I looked into a large, even palatial, room.

General Dudayev sat inside. He rose to greet us. I had expected a towering giant but shook hands with someone only marginally taller than me. I sat down. General Dudayev returned to his swivel chair, positioned in front of a simple wooden desk. The general was in military dress and wore shoes so well shined that I thought I might see my reflection if I bent to inspect them more closely. His jet black hair lay neatly pomaded and parted at the side. I wondered if it was by coincidence or design that his groomed mustache resembled the wings of an airplane. I knew that he had only recently resigned from his position as a general in the Soviet air force. I suspected he still wore his old uniform. A broad-brimmed air force hat lay by the phone on his otherwise empty desk.

In his new position, General Dudayev tried to unite everyone in the Caucasus in a holy war against Russia. I thought he might be mercurial, so I had prepared easy questions designed to build trust before I asked difficult ones. In no mood for small talk, the general interrupted with an attack against Yeltsin.

"If Yeltsin continues his high-handed tactics, we'll launch a terror campaign in Moscow. There will be bombs in the Moscow metro system and a nuclear plant near Moscow will be blown up."

Although this could be dismissed as a blustery threat, he seemed quite serious in intent. I asked questions in a neutral tone, received more information and then understood the interview would end. Before it did, I asked the general if I could take his picture. He seemed pleased.

Later that day, I walked through the square. There seemed to be even more men with guns packed into it than the day before. I returned to the secretary's office, but no one was there. I wandered the corridors in search of information. The crack of gunshot echoed outside. Cheers just meant more shots fired in the air. I saw a man in a fur hat and an old woman, a babushka, who wore a black dress and matching black headscarf, in one room. I went in. A Kalashnikov lay across a bare wooden desk. A man poked his head in the door and said the Russian Parliament had rejected the state of emergency imposed by President Yeltsin. Then he ran off down the hall. I turned to the man in the hat and asked, "When did this happen?"

"This is the first we've heard of it," the hatted man whooped.

"Cowards, infidels, they've run away with their tails between their legs," I think the babushka shouted. The old woman, a black mass, lunged for the Kalashnikov. My heart raced. I dove under the table. Safe there, I peered up to see the babushka raise the Kalashnikov straight up in the air, toward the ceiling.

"Wait, wait," the man in the fur hat said. I expected him to grab the gun, but he grabbed the babushka's elbow instead. He gently guided her, gun still upright, her finger still on the trigger, toward the window and pointed the barrel straight out.

"Go ahead now, go ahead," he said.

The babushka pulled the trigger. Several shots rang out. She pulled herself away from the window and laughed. Then she roared "we won" and something about a wet chicken, which I took to mean, "Those Russians are made of jelly."

That was how my knees felt. I slid out from under the table and stood up. I said goodbye and left. I still heard gunshot from the streets, so I lurked in the corridors for some time until

I heard (near) silence again. On my way back to the hotel, I checked the sidewalk for traces of blood. As far as I could see, no one had been hit.

A huge crowd descended on the airport. So many passengers were desperate to leave after spending days trapped in Grozny. Stephen and I got lucky and obtained tickets for the first flight out. Safely in my seat, I buckled up and reclined. I shut my eyes and thought about guns. They felt almost as unreal now as they had in Ottawa when I was a child.

I remembered a story that my father told me about his early days of military training during the Second World War. Instructors took my father and other recruits to a rocky beach for a combat exercise. The instructors played the part of the enemy and told the recruits they would shoot at them from cliffs above the beach. When my father and his friends ran toward a designated safe spot, bullets ricocheted off rocks near their feet. "I was madder than blazes," my father said. "We expected them to fire blanks, not live ammunition." He never took a gun for granted again. Maybe someone needed to fire at me before I could feel that too.

7

VADYM

When I arrived back in Kiev, Toronto Marta called.

"How was it?" she asked.

"The Russian troops pulled back, and I don't think anyone was hurt."

"Chechnya's one place I'd never want to go," she said. I understood. I thought the same before but now that I had been to a conflict zone and seen guns, I almost felt proud.

Marta switched topics. "The parliamentary committee investigating the coup has apparently discovered interesting information," she said. It took me a minute to forget Chechnya and focus on Ukrainian politics.

"Is Vadym on that committee?" I asked.

"He is," Marta replied.

"I heard he's making a documentary about who supported the coup. I wonder if it'll be censored."

"Not if Vadym's good at his job," Marta joked. "He's also heading up a press freedom committee." I made a mental note to ask Lesyia what she knew. She and Vadym remained close friends. Even though he was a Member of Parliament, he worked on TV documentaries, was still a journalist, one of us, and generous with information. Coup talk reminded me of the referendum on Ukrainian independence.

"I can't believe the referendum's in less than two weeks," I said. "Do you think there's any chance of a vote against independence?"

"No way," Marta insisted. I agreed.

When the votes were counted, Ukrainians overwhelmingly confirmed Parliament's vote for independence and elected Leonid Kravchuk the first president of Ukraine. Marta and I celebrated with friends at a local hotel. Our tables sagged under the weight of so many bottles of vodka and cognac, platters of caviar, kovbasa, cheese, pickles, varenyky, Chicken Kiev and every other celebratory dish. Rukh politicians, our waiters, journalists and various passersby linked arms in a huge circle under blue and yellow banners and balloons and sang the national anthem, "Ukraine Has Still Not Died."

A few days later, I boarded a flight for Minsk. When we landed, I stood on the tarmac at the airport in Minsk with other journalists. We waited to find out whether the Soviet Union would survive. Yeltsin, Kravchuk and the Belarussian leader Stanislav Shushkevitch were conferring at a Belarussian lodge in Belavezhskaya Pushcha, near the Polish border. I gossiped with my colleagues, but really my head spun. We all believed rumours that they would dissolve the Soviet Union. Everything I had studied about a seamless Soviet state, one where no ethnic group had nationalist aspirations, and one common language was spoken by all, seemed a sham. When the leaders arrived back in Minsk, they confirmed what we suspected. They declared the Soviet Union dead, which meant

Mikhail Gorbachev would be politically irrelevant. A new order would begin, a Commonwealth of Independent States.

I watched an interview with Gorbachev that night on TV. His expression revealed more than his words. He looked so betrayed. I wondered if Gorbachev still believed that version of Soviet history I had been taught and once believed too.

I had already had time to adjust to changes. Since the August declaration of independence I had thought of Ukraine as a separate country, though one undergoing a complex transition. Ukraine needed to build many independent institutions of its own, free from Moscow's control. Banking was so rudimentary here. Most business seemed transacted through cash, barter and bribes. Still, I felt a sense of history in the making on Christmas Day when I watched Gorbachev formally resign. By the end of the year, the Soviet Union no longer existed. I wondered what would happen next.

In early January 1992, I sat at the desk in my small study and looked out the window over the treetops. Snowflakes swirled in the sky. I hoped this wind would chase the grey clouds away. I could not remember the last time we had seen sunshine in Kiev.

The shrill ring of the phone roused me into action. I picked up the handset and shifted. I sat on the top step of a short staircase that led down into the kitchen area and said hello in English.

"May I speak to Susan?" a man asked in a North American accent.

"Speaking." The man's voice did not sound familiar. He introduced himself as a businessman, Mr. Smith, on assignment in Kiev. He spoke for a few minutes and then said, "I have some information that will interest you." I asked for details, but he would provide none over the telephone.

"I'm staying at the Zhovtnevyi Hotel. Meet me here." I had no reason to trust this stranger. He established no common link through friends or acquaintances and barely stated his business. I hesitated but did agree to go. Foreigners, still rare enough in Kiev for interest, had never posed a threat. I wondered what this man wanted and who had given him my number.

I lived so centrally that I could reach the hotel quickly on foot. I scratched at frost built up on one window pane in my study. I pressed my hand against the glass and felt the sharp sting of January cold. I decided I would drive.

I took two coats from the cupboard and put them on, layering one on top of the other. I lifted a square hat, the shape of a cake box, from one shelf and placed it on my head. I pulled on wool socks and boots, slid my hands into thick lined gloves and stepped into the corridor. I fished a set of impossibly long keys from my pocket, locked the door and then waited for the arrival of the elevator. A couple fit inside with moderate ease; three was a squeeze. I stared at a jagged hole in the door on the slow ride down and wondered, as I always did, if a bullet had made the hole.

A snowdrift partially blocked the door. I shoved hard, opened it and blinked as I emerged from our windowless lobby into the courtyard. I tramped through snow that reached my knees. Some spilled in over the top of my boots. As I reached the street the warmth that I carried from my well-heated flat dissipated. I felt the first burst of cold sting my thighs. I moved as quickly as I could on the snowy sidewalks to reach a *stoyanka* – a guarded parking lot – just above October Revolution, no Independence Square. I was still adjusting to new names for streets and other city landmarks.

I had kept my red hatchback Lada in these guarded lots since the morning that I woke and found it stripped of all exterior parts, left wheel-less, propped up on wooden blocks. Street parking was no longer safe. I had ignored warnings not to leave my car out and so could blame no one but myself.

I felt moisture build inside the scarf wrapped tightly around my face. I soon reached the lot and my car, opened the door and started the engine. I took a snow brush from the trunk and cleaned off my nearly buried car. When I had finished, I knocked the brush clean and put it away. I opened the door and sat on the driver's seat. The heater had warmed the interior quickly. This one part of my Lada worked well. I put my hands in front of the vents to warm them in a blast of hot air and wondered about a faintly salty, fishy smell inside the car.

I looked in the back seat and noticed a package wrapped in newspaper. I picked it up and unfurled the paper. A dried fish dropped out. Evgenyi, I thought. He'd taken to leaving small presents in my car. I turned the ignition off and went to a cabin at the edge of the lot. Evgenyi, the *stoyanka* attendant, saw me as I approached the booth. He flung the door open.

"Well, look who's here!" he said. I wished him Happy New Year and thanked him for the fish.

"Come in for a New Year's toast," he insisted.

"I'm driving," I said. "But I'd love a cup of tea," I added as I scrambled in from the cold. I sat on a tiny stool as Evgenyi made tea for me and poured a shot of vodka for himself. He inquired about my family in Canada and I asked him how he had spent the holidays.

"Alone with my thoughts," he said. I explained that I was late for a meeting and edged toward the door.

"Sit for a while," he insisted. "Do you know about Stalin?" I nodded. I had studied Stalin's regime in university. So many innocent people died. Purges resulted in mass arrests, show trials and sentences in the Gulag. Sometimes guards just shot their prisoners in the back of the head.

"I was a driver back then. I didn't do any of the dirty work," he said. I wanted to end this conversation. I could not bear to hear more. I already imagined Evgenyi behind the wheel as agents pushed victims into the car for their trip to the security services headquarters. Interrogation, torture and sentencing would follow.

"Those guys in the service were my family, my brothers," he said. I wanted to shout, "Why tell me this?" But I sat silent, uncomfortable. I guessed he felt safe talking to a foreigner who might not judge him. Maybe he would die soon and needed to unburden himself. I edged toward the door again. He put up his hand as if to say wait, so I did. He rummaged in a drawer and pulled a pin out.

"It's my badge for service," he said and put it in my hand. "A gift, for the New Year."

I smiled and thanked him but felt quite horrified by my gift, as if someone from the SS had just handed me Nazi memorabilia.

"I must go now," I insisted. "I'm very late." He opened the door. I ran back to my car.

When I reached the hotel, I parked and fumbled in my pocket for the notebook where I had recorded Mr. Smith's room number. I also pulled out Evgenyi's badge and shoved it in the bottom of my bag. I sat in the car for a few minutes to reflect on what he had told me, compose myself and switch gears for this next meeting. When I felt ready, I entered the lobby and rode the elevator up. I knocked on Mr. Smith's door. A man in casual business dress opened it and asked me in. Papers lay strewn across a small desk. I sat on a chair nearby.

"I'm sure you're wondering why I invited you here," he said. I did.

"Do you cover business stories?" he asked. I said that under Communism the government had only permitted small-scale experimentation with private business, usually restaurants or cafés.

"Well get ready for some changes. I've worked for several months on a big telecommunications deal and I don't like what I see." Few people in Ukraine had a phone. There would be a good market for any company that was able to meet this demand. I asked for details.

"I lost the deal. I have no doubt at all those guys that won paid a significant bribe," Mr. Smith said.

I felt shocked by what Evgenyi had told me but not by what Mr. Smith said. Deals worked that way here, so payment of a bribe seemed a reasonable assumption. I had learned how the market in Ukraine functioned through a gas station attendant not long after I arrived, when Ukraine was still Communist. As a foreigner I received no coupons that would allow me to purchase gasoline at state-run stations. A co-operative station, a semi-private enterprise, opened, and this is where I bought gas. Usually the line stretched several blocks down the street and the wait was several hours. Demand always exceeded supply and at some point gas ran out.

A group of boys – the oldest, about fourteen – learned to work the system. Several joined the line with canisters. When one got gas, he would walk down the line of cars from the back and auction his tin to the highest bidder. Initially I resisted buying from the boys, however, soon I became a loyal customer.

One day I arrived at the station and saw no line. As I drove closer to the pump, I noticed a small handwritten sign posted on it that said No Gas. I had lived in Ukraine long enough to realize that No Gas might mean "gas only under the right circumstances." I saw a babushka wrapped in a heavy coat inside a kiosk by the pump. I opened the trunk of my car and pulled out a bottle of vodka. I walked over to the kiosk and knocked on the glass. The woman saw me and the bottle. She opened her window.

"Is there any gas?" I asked.

"Is there any vodka?" she countered. We reached a deal. Then I asked the woman how she got her job.

"I bought it, of course. I had to borrow the money."

"So you pay it back with deals like this?"

"Girl, tell me how else?" Whoever controlled the telephone system likely played by the same rules that had existed under Communism. I was not that interested in Mr. Smith's story, but he still told me more.

Soon documents lay across the table. We stood side by side as he pieced together a complex puzzle of secret meetings, mostly in overseas locations like Switzerland, where Mr. Smith alleged that foreign company representatives gave more than a million dollars in cash to high-ranking Ukrainian officials in exchange for business support.

"How did you obtain this information?"

"I have my contacts," he said. "You should investigate this." I felt suspicious about what he had told me and wondered if Mr. Smith wanted revenge and was trying to use me to get it.

"Do you think this is linked to the coup?" I asked.

"Yes," he said, "to regime change. You need political guarantees to do business here, to secure the market. Before independence those guarantees came from politicians in Moscow. Now politicians in Kiev have that power."

"So did you offer them money?" I asked.

"No. I explained how the deal could help the economy boom and bring more business here," the man said. "But it was clear they had something of more personal benefit in mind. No one stated this, but they wanted a bribe. Those guys who won the deal must have paid it."

Mr. Smith had tracked his rivals' movements throughout the fall. I found this odd, almost obsessive. Inexperienced in business, I wondered if large corporations commonly behaved this way. I left armed with ammunition for an investigative story but felt unnerved. It would be a serious matter to probe allegations of corruption so high up. This encounter reminded me of that sinister undercurrent from my early days in Kiev. Even though Ukraine was independent, the same men remained in power as before.

Days passed. I made a few calls but did little more to substantiate Mr. Smith's claim. I did not exactly forget what he told me, but focused on other stories instead. This investigation would take time and I wasn't convinced it was worth the effort or risk.

One morning in mid-February, the telephone rang. The answering machine intercepted the call before I reached the phone. I had just arrived home on a 4 a.m. flight from Crimea and lay tired in bed, still groggy from so little sleep. I heard Mary's voice over the answering machine. She said something about Vadym Boyko. I managed to grab the phone handset before Mary hung up.

"Have you heard about Vadym?" she said.

"No, what happened?"

"He's dead."

Dead? I turned the word over in my mind, stunned by the news but still detached. Sadness had yet to set in. I tried hard to process information that I did not want. Mary told me what she knew. The previous night a journalist friend, Marko, had received a call about a fire in Vadym's apartment and a dead body. The caller said the body was believed to be Vadym's and asked Marko to come and identify it. Marko asked a friend, Ilko, to accompany him. In the apartment Marko and Ilko saw Vadym sprawled across the floor, his torso and face were badly burned. The description nearly made me retch. I could not imagine having to view the semi-charred corpse of a friend.

"Who did it?" I asked.

"They say his television set exploded. We'll get together this morning and see what we can do," Mary said.

We would meet at New York Marta's news bureau in the building next door. As I dressed, I thought of Vadym and one of my earliest meetings with him at the Ukrainian State Television and Radio Headquarters. He rushed down the steps, casually elegant: slim, in black jeans and a maroon sweatshirt, with that glossy dark hair. He held a bundle of paper and stopped to show me what it contained.

"There's more crossed out than left in," Vadym joked. I did not understand what Vadym meant until I leafed through the bundle. I saw a heavily edited evening newscast script, with large sections of text blacked out.

"At least this guy still has integrity," Vadym said. "The worst is self-censorship, when a script is handed in and comes back clean."

I left my building, walked through the courtyard, under the archway, up the street and entered the next building, climbing the stairs in semi-darkness. Dull light filtered in from a window far above.

I entered the news bureau. Some people sat in chairs, others stood, huddled in clusters. Our host, New York Marta, who had recently returned to Kiev, was usually so cheerful and optimistic. She looked sombre now. Mary talked to the friends, Ilko and Marko, who had identified Vadym's body. Lesyia, sat quietly. She was in shock. She had had the closest relationship with Vadym. Serhyi, one of Vadym and Lesyia's close friends, who was also an MP, stood near Lesyia.

None of us wanted to be alone. We formed a circle in the main room and exchanged information. No one believed that Vadym had died in an accident caused by an exploding television set. He'd last been seen the day before his death.

Ilko and Marko had arrived at Vadym's apartment just after firefighters extinguished the blaze. People were already swarming inside his apartment. They touched items that could be evidence and potentially destroyed important clues.

"A crime scene like this should have been sealed off," Ilko said. But the investigator in charge did not bother to take samples or conduct interviews with friends or neighbours in the building. He stood near the door and told everybody who came in that Vadym, a television reporter and advocate of uncensored, free media, had died in an accident caused when his own television set exploded. Ilko and Marko described the gutted, scorched interior of the apartment. The position of Vadym's body, the pattern of his burns and the intensity of the fire all suggested a different version of events.

Ilko and Marko questioned neighbours. One had heard a blast from Vadym's apartment and investigated. He pushed the door open with a ruler because he was afraid that there might be another explosion. This detail troubled Serhyi; he said that Vadym always locked his apartment door. Serhyi felt even more disturbed when firefighters told him they had to break into Vadym's apartment. This meant that two eyewitness accounts — one from the neighbour and one from the firefighters — were contradictory. The neighbour also said that he saw an athletic blond young man enter Vadym's apartment. He opened the door with a key. We had half a dozen fragments of information but none fit together in a pattern that made sense.

One of our acquaintances received a phone call from a contact, a lab technician with access to forensic evidence. The contact insisted Vadym did not have smoke in his lungs. This suggested that he died before fire broke out in his apartment. We speculated that someone might have killed him and then drenched his body in gasoline and set it alight.

As the days passed, we all searched for clues but did not learn much more. Lesyia and I went to Vadym's apartment. It was a painful visit, especially for her. Lesyia knew the way well. I had never been before.

Vadym lived in a modern concrete block high-rise, so ordinary, not a place for murder. We climbed the stairs to his apartment, the red stencilled "2B" still visible in a patch of white beneath the scorched door. Paint peeled away, melted by intense heat from the fire. A note lay on the threshold with some red carnations, a candle and a red sash. Others had come before us to say their goodbyes as we did now. Lesyia and I stood in silence for some time.

Then we left the building and looked at Vadym's apartment from outside. A long trail of soot stretched four floors up from his windows, a black marker of death. Plywood replaced shattered glass in one window frame. His apartment was boarded up and abandoned; all life was gone from this place.

We noticed a large rubbish container outside the building. Lesyia recognized some of Vadym's belongings, half-burned pages from his copy of *The Maltese Falcon*. I clambered up the container and leaned in. I pulled out a page, hopeful for anything that might, however unlikely, one day provide evidence to unravel this mystery. I could not believe a faulty TV had caused such an intense fire and a horrible death.

I called my parents. I wanted a connection to home, a place where I felt safe. My father answered the phone. I could not explain what I needed but felt soothed by his voice. We discussed those small events, mundane for others but not for us, that made up daily life at home. He spoke about the latest antics of our family dog. I told my father the story of Vadym's death and heard from this intelligent, grounded man, a lawyer who thought rationally, how unlikely it would be for someone to die through a malfunctioning TV.

In Kiev, rumours swirled. Because he was handsome, Vadym had always attracted a lot of male and female attention. I heard speculation about a crime of passion – a romantic entanglement that prompted jealous rage and a brutal attack. Others traced his death to the coup. They remembered Vadym's investigation into who in Ukraine had supported the Moscow coup plotters and thought someone afraid of exposure had arranged his murder.

In a press conference with Leonid Kravchuk soon after Vadym's death, one journalist put the question bluntly: "Boyko's death, was this an accident or a political murder?" Kravchuk replied, "All the information that I have had so far points to a tragic accident." He said that the forensic evidence and injuries were consistent with those that could be inflicted by a television set that exploded.

"If that is true, we'll have to come out with a number of measures that would rule out the possibility of such accidents in the future," Kravchuk added. I left the news conference full of doubt.

In the days that followed, I juggled my usual reporting duties but still thought about Vadym. I could not accept that so many questions remained unanswered. I bumped into Mary in Parliament. I wanted to talk about Vadym's case with her, but she had no updates and seemed very excited, her mind clearly on something else.

"I think I just got permission to go to a nuclear bomber base," she said. "Are you interested in coming?"

"Where is it and what do you mean you *think* you have permission, don't you need a permit?" I asked.

"Uzyn." Then she named a military man whom I did not know and said "He telephoned my name through to the base. How about giving it a try before he changes his mind? He could add your name to the list."

"Is that Bashkirov's base?" I asked

"Yes, and 70 percent of the servicemen on the base just swore the oath of allegiance to Ukraine," she said. "This is serious stuff. It's the first strategic forces division to swear allegiance."

I had been surprised, like so many other people, when news first broke that Bashkirov, a major general in command of the Ukrainian Uzyn base, had disobeyed an order from Moscow to land his plane in Russia and instead flew back to his base in Ukraine. When Bashkirov arrived safely in Uzyn, he swore an oath of loyalty to Ukraine and now nearly his whole base stood behind him. We all wondered if Russia would retaliate. There had already been so much tension between Russia and Ukraine over who would control the Black Sea Fleet in Crimea and now, this. Of course I wanted to go. It would be an opportunity to assess whether Russia and Ukraine might actually go to war over division of their military assets and their states.

"Sure," I said. "I'll get my car and pick you up in an hour."

On the way to the *stoyanka*, I remembered one problem. My headlights had burned out and I had not been able to find replacement bulbs. If only Evgenyi left those as presents instead of dried-up fish. When I returned to pick up Mary, others stood with her on the sidewalk—Toronto Marta, Stephen and Sasha, who interpreted for Stephen and me.

"We're all going," Mary said cheerfully. As everyone squeezed in and buckled up, I mentioned the problem with my headlights.

"Don't worry, we'll be back long before dark," Mary said.

When we arrived at the base, Mary spoke to the guard and mentioned the name of the general who was supposed to have called with permission for us to visit. The guard raised the barrier and waved us through. There could be no better sign. We had entered a nuclear bomber base, a place strictly off limits weeks ago. I saw planes in the distance and tried to move closer. Before I got far, a minder appeared. Once in the main building, he shooed us down a corridor and into a room.

"Please wait here," our minder said. He locked the door behind him. We waited patiently. Our trip was spontaneous. Base personnel must need time to find us a guide.

One hour passed, then a second hour. Stephen tried the door. "Still locked," he said.

"Do you think we're under arrest, or detention?" I asked. We waited longer. Another hour passed. Stephen and I practised our Ukrainian. Sasha, ever dapper and patient, coached us.

Every half-hour or so our minder, a lieutenant colonel, kept appearing with new excuses as to why we should remain locked in the room. He told us at different times that Major General Bashkirov was not on the base, then that he was on the base but could not meet us, and finally, that he had left.

"Pictures?" Toronto Marta suggested. "At least we can record our trip." We perched on a windowsill and posed. Then we waited quietly as more time passed. I thought of Vadym.

In his case, just like this one, we sensed there was something important to discover just beyond our reach but we were so easily shut out.

Evening fell. Eventually our minder came back again.

"I have to go the bathroom," Marta said to him. He unlocked the door and allowed her out. Within seconds she came racing back.

"Bashkirov, he's here," she shouted. We ran out of the room and down the hallway toward a group of military men a short distance away. The general was polite. We asked questions, but he provided no answers of real news value. Then we were escorted off the base.

It was dark now. With no headlights, I drove slowly down a pitch-black country highway. I could not see where the road ended and the ditch began. Mary hung out the passenger window, trying to prevent me from driving off the road.

"Left," she shouted. "Left again." Eventually we flagged down a truck and paid the driver to go slowly so we could piggyback on his tail lights.

When I arrived home, tired from the strain of the drive, I listened to the messages on my answering machine. Mr. Smith had called again. He'd already tried a few times. I did not want to speak to him. More days passed. My conscience nagged. Eventually I returned his call. We met at his hotel. I sat in the same armchair as before.

"Vadym investigated the telecommunications deal," he said. I felt a shiver of alarm, but only a shiver. So many rumours surrounded Vadym's death already. I did not know what to believe.

"I'm sure they killed him because of this and you need to be careful," Mr. Smith said. "I saw Vadym not long before he died. He told me that he had all the evidence and would publicize the facts."

I left the hotel more confused than ever, unnerved, a little ashamed too. Vadym followed up on Mr. Smith's story while I merely toyed with it and uncovered little of substance. A better journalist would find proof that either substantiated Mr. Smith's claim or disproved it – would add one more piece of evidence to Vadym's case or eliminate one rumoured reason for his death. I did neither.

Around this time, I received a call from the procurator's office. The office wanted to interview me as part of an investigation into Vadym's case. My bitter feelings had subsided; I felt hopeful now.

On the day of the appointment, I walked up to the procurator's office and told the authorities all that I knew. I gave a statement but received little information in exchange. In fact, I left with the impression that no investigation would ensue. I felt a wave of paranoia as I had during my early days in Kiev and wondered if the purpose of the interview was simply to ensure that I did not know too much, which I did not. That sense of unease intensified on my walk home. I understood so little of what really occurred in Ukraine. The best we could hope for with Vadym's case, I thought, was that someday someone would feel the need to confess.

8

MOLDOVA

"Susie bear, do you have a funnel?" Bill asked. We stood in March sunshine on the road outside his apartment, just around the corner from mine.

I did. I also had several extra canisters for gasoline. Bill and I had phoned our gasoline contacts (I now purchased mine from the trunk of a local taxi driver) and pooled our resources. We knew that it would be hard to find fuel along the way, so we carried enough with us for our return trip. We were going to Moldova, which bordered Ukraine. I thought of Moldova as my turf. I had been there before, staked a claim, and would now return to cover a story that I considered mine.

"I hope we see a big hairy Cossack," Bill said.

"I'm sure we will. I read that at least 150 are already there," I replied. "A lot of the Russian Cossacks seem to be Afghan vets."

"It's Cossacks and Transdniestrians against the Moldovans. I guess the Russian army based in Trans-Dniester will be the deciding factor," Bill said. We discussed possible outcomes for this conflict in Moldova that pitted ethnic Russians in Trans-Dniester (a region of Moldova) against the Moldovan majority. The two sides were separated by a river, the Dniester. Reports that Russian Cossacks had snuck into Moldova to support the Transdniestrians intrigued us.

"Last time I was there, the Transdniestrians thought the Moldovans were getting ready to unite with Romania," I said. "They called the Moldovans *Romanians*." Distracted, Bill said, "just a sec." He rushed into his apartment.

"We'd better bring this," he insisted as he came running back out. He waved a long, floppy rubber tube, a siphon.

"Oh no," I groaned. Whoever used the siphon would end up with a mouthful of gas.

"Don't worry, I'll do it if we need to," Bill said.

We packed vodka – no better currency for barter – and some food, but canisters of gasoline took up most of the room in the trunk. I thought briefly about the possibility that if rear-ended, we might blow up like a bomb on four wheels. Once we had finished loading the car, we set off. We travelled southwest toward the Moldovan border. I enjoyed the company, the scenery and the sense of freedom I always felt on long trips by car. I did not enjoy the road conditions, especially once we veered off the main highway and travelled along increasingly potholed tracks that could barely be called roads.

"I wanted to be a race car driver," Bill shouted as he zigzagged at top speed past potholes, several of which were large enough to swallow us and the car. The odd time he accidentally dipped into one, my teeth clacked and my body banged against the door. I wondered if my Lada would shed parts along the way. We reached the Moldovan border and sailed through on our final leg of the trip to Tiraspol, the capital of Transdniestria.

"Look up there. What's he got on?" Bill asked as we approached a driving school just outside Tiraspol. I looked at a man who stood by the school. He wore a faded military jacket that was different from any I'd seen before and baggy pantaloons. He held a long whip.

"That must be a Cossack," said Bill, excited now. He pulled into the school parking lot. Once inside the building, we realized the Cossacks had turned the school into their headquarters.

A busy barber was cutting men's hair in the hallway. I stopped in front of a small shrine set up in memory of a twenty-one-year-old Russian Cossack, who had recently been killed. His black and white photograph formed the centrepiece. A black funeral sash was stretched diagonally across the frame. This Cossack looked too robust and young for death. I wondered what had motivated him to come here and risk dying so far away from home.

I moved away from the shrine, struck by the raucous force of life that permeated other parts of the headquarters. Most Cossacks, shaggy-headed and needing a trim, lounged around and opened beer bottles with the bayonets on the end of their rifles. Several taped syringes to their rifles and stuffed their pockets with bandages so that they would have first aid supplies at hand if they were wounded.

A large man in a mismatched uniform approached me. He said that he came from Irkutsk. Siberia was so far away.

"Why are you here?" I asked him.

"To defend our brother Slavs. They're under attack. We'll protect them," he said.

"But we're not in Russia. This is Moldova," I said.

"These are our people and this is our land. They won't take it from us," he angrily insisted. I pointed to the shrine set up for the young Cossack and asked how he had died.

"We had no guns when we arrived," the Siberian Cossack said. "We armed ourselves with planks of wood." I thought of the square in Grozny where men without guns had done the same. I felt disturbed that an item I associated with carpentry, maybe a board for a bookshelf, could so easily become a weapon.

"We captured guns from the Moldovans," the Siberian Cossack explained. "The Transdniestrians gave us more." I asked if by Transdniestrians he meant the Russian army stationed here but could extract no information from him on this point. Officially, the army remained neutral.

I felt insecure in this driving school turned Cossack headquarters. The disorderliness that bordered on chaos unnerved me, as did the abundance of weapons and alcohol. I did not think that vodka, beer and guns should ever mix.

I went to find Bill. I wanted to leave. He spoke with Mikhail, the Cossack whom we had seen standing outside.

"Don't worry," Mikhail said. "Any Cossack who shows up drunk for battle gets ten lashes from this," he said and cracked his whip. Bill finished the interview. Then we left and drove into Tiraspol. We saw Lenin statues and hammers and sickles everywhere.

"It's a Soviet theme park," Bill said. "Didn't anyone tell them the Soviet Union doesn't exist anymore?" I felt a pang of nostalgia as we approached Parliament. A tall red granite statue of Lenin still stood on a plinth in front of the building.

"Doesn't that remind you of the Lenin in October Revolution Square?"

"Kiev's is way bigger. I researched it for a feature. Kiev's Lenin weighs a thousand tons. City councillors thought they might blow it up but found out that the monument was connected to the subway station below," Bill told me. "They also considered firing acid pellets to dissolve it.

"Seriously?" Bill nodded.

I lived close by what had been October Revolution Square and was now Independence Square. Workers had chipped away at Lenin with pneumatic drills for months. They had also dismantled metal figures at his base. A crane poked up from beside the base. Some nights sparks had cascaded down the front of the monument, orange fireflies against an indigo sky, as workers sawed Lenin and his comrades apart. One by one, they were carted away.

We stopped at Igor Smirnov's office. I'd been there before when he was a Communist official in the Soviet Union. Now Transdniestrians considered him their president. No one in the office would acknowledge Moldovan independence, Moscow loyalties were still strong. Lenin's portrait hung on the walls. Most rooms were still festooned with Soviet symbols.

"I'm not sure if this is possible, but I think it's even more Soviet in there than before," I said to Bill as we left.

"I sense Russia is trying to make this place one of their outposts. Maybe Russians are reconciled to losing the rest of Moldova but want Trans-Dniester as a military base on the Western Front," he said.

"And they're getting the Cossacks to fight and die for them," I added. "Not that they need much encouragement. Did you hear Mikhail say, 'This is our holy land,' just before we left?" Bill nodded that he had.

We took a bridge over the Dniester River and drove to Chisinau, the Moldovan capital, for interviews on the other side. I looked forward to checking into our hotel after such a long day. As I lay on my bed and flipped through my notes, I heard people in the hallway who spoke with English accents. I stepped out of my room and met three English journalists in the corridor. Two were based in Romania. The third, a pretty young woman with long blonde hair, fine features and the voice of a British royal, was their friend who was visiting from England.

"Charlotte," she said by way of introduction. "Have you met the Cossacks yet?"

"Yes, we've just spent the afternoon with them. Have you been here long?"

I really wanted to ask, Why are you here? Don't you know that stories in former Soviet republics belong to journalists based in the former Soviet Union? But I minded my manners and kept my mouth shut.

"Just arrived," Charlotte replied. "I'm working on a feature now. A lot of these Cossacks trace their history back to the sixteenth century, to the Don Cossack state. They defended Russia from Mongol and Tatar raids." I felt embarrassed that she had better information than me. The Siberian Cossack I interviewed told me that he had inherited his uniform, but I hadn't probed him on his family history. Charlotte clearly had.

Bill came into the corridor to discuss dinner plans.

"You're already dressed for it I see," Bill noted and complimented Charlotte on her skirt.

"These are my work clothes." Charlotte said. "Think of the British Empire. Skirts were good enough for women explorers back then, so why not now?" I stared down at my wrinkled shirt and black jeans. She had made an interesting point. I liked Charlotte and set aside territorial concerns. I learned more about Charlotte that night over dinner. She had worked for the *Daily Mail* but now studied at Oxford and was in Moldova on holiday before returning to Oxford to write her final exams.

The next day Charlotte, a male companion and I decided to return to Tiraspol for more interviews. When we reached the bridge over the Dniester River that Bill and I had crossed freely by car, we saw a barricade and checkpoints – a low wall of concrete blocks guarded by eight soldiers with automatic rifles. We pulled over and approached the soldiers on foot.

"May we cross?" I asked one.

"Papers," he said. We handed the soldiers our accreditation papers and waited. He examined each stamp carefully. "We can't guarantee how they'll respond," the soldier said as he gestured at the checkpoint on the opposite end of the bridge. "You should walk. They might shoot at a car." We passed through the checkpoint and stepped onto the bridge. Charlotte and I led the way. Our male companion walked behind us.

"A soldier won't fire at women," he said. I hoped the sentries on the other side weren't drunken Cossacks. As we approached the mid-point of the bridge, I could see that one was watching us through his field glasses. I felt exposed and vulnerable.

I thought of a trip I had made with Sallie from Hungary to Romania just after the Romanian revolution in January 1990. Curfew rules forbade road traffic after dark. We misjudged the time and raced back at dusk. A light swayed ahead on the road. We thought it was a lantern on a donkey cart. We realized our mistake as we flew past a guard at a checkpoint. He waved a flashlight. Sallie, who drove, slammed on the brakes. She reversed. The guard had already raised his gun.

"I would have shot you if you hadn't stopped," he shouted. We made peace with leftover gifts that we carried – cigarettes from Sallie, Coca-Cola from me.

As we walked slowly across the bridge, I thought it must be so easy to be killed by accident in war. This time I watched carefully for gestures made by the sentry, especially any sign that he might raise his gun.

When we actually heard gunshot, Charlotte reacted, not me. We were interviewing a Transdniestrian official in his Tiraspol office. Nothing bad had happened in Grozny, so I paid no attention to the pop of a gun in the street. Charlotte, who knew better, ducked to the floor.

"Ours," the official said. We finished the interview and crossed back over the bridge that divided "us" from "them."

It had been three months since the Soviet Union had officially dissolved. Ukraine, Moldova, Russia and the other Soviet republics were all independent, but people still probed boundaries. The Chechens and Transdniestrians went the furthest. Chechnya tried to secede from Russia and Trans-Dniester wanted to break away from Moldova. Friends and I tested borders too. We travelled as far and as quickly as possible. The Soviet visa regime no longer existed. We suspected that newly independent states would soon enforce their own rules, but there was flexibility for now. I invited Charlotte to join friends and me on a trip to Central Asia.

"I don't have visas for any of those countries," she said.

"Well, let's just see what happens," I replied.

I bought Charlotte a ticket to Uzbekistan with no request from the agent to see a visa. Booking into Central Asian hotels was just as easy. Woohooo! That's what I felt as we journeyed thousands of miles across several time zones for mere dollars and with no trouble. I had never felt so free. When we arrived back in Kiev, Charlotte did not want to leave but had to return home for university exams. She would travel to Bucharest (via Chisinau), where she would catch her flight for London. We discussed her travel plans in my kitchen.

"I'll accompany you as far as Chisinau," I told her.

"Really," she shouted from the top of a stepladder. "That would be lovely." She wore a brightly coloured stripy silk nightgown and draped reams of the same material over curtain rods mounted over the balcony door. The material was a souvenir from our Central Asia trip.

"Much better," she said as she climbed down the ladder and eyed her makeshift drapes. I no longer thought of Charlotte as competition from Romania. She was one of us and I wanted to help her get home to England.

"When's your flight?" I asked.

"I'll double-check, but I think it's next Wednesday," she said.

"It might be easiest to take the train to Odessa and catch a taxi from there for Chisinau. Will you be all right the rest of the way to Bucharest on your own?" She said yes and we agreed on this plan.

Over the next few days, I checked the wires for news from Moldova and saw nothing of note. We planned our trip with time for interviews in Chisinau. A few days before Charlotte's flight from Bucharest, we boarded the overnight Kiev-Odessa express. We arrived in Odessa on schedule the next morning. We slid our cabin door open, walked along the narrow train corridor and climbed down a short set of metal steps to the platform.

I found a taxi driver near the station entrance.

"Odessa-Chisinau, how much?" I asked.

"Fifty dollars," the driver replied.

"What!" I thought a normal rate might be ten. I interrogated him but obtained no specific information that could justify such a big jump in price. The next driver I approached refused to take us to Moldova. Several others also said no. I suspected they did not want the hassle of crossing a border. I negotiated with the first driver. We eventually agreed on a forty-dollar fare.

Our taciturn driver ignored our attempts to start a conversation with him. Charlotte and I sat and chatted in the back seat.

We watched countryside fly by as we sped along the road, over the border into Trans-Dniester. We reached Tiraspol quickly. The driver stopped at a local Intourist hotel.

"Why have we stopped here?" I asked.

"This is as far as I'll go."

"But we negotiated a fare to Chisinau."

"You can catch another taxi from here." I felt my jaw tighten and my pulse rate quicken. I translated for Charlotte.

"Whaat! It's not that much farther on. He's only got to get us across the bridge and go on for a bit." I argued with the driver. He would not budge and demanded the fare. He had already put our bags on the sidewalk near the hotel entrance.

"It's no use," I told Charlotte. "Let's just get another car." We reluctantly paid the driver. He sped off. We looked for a taxi, but the streets by the hotel seemed deserted.

"Shall we check in here tonight and leave for Chisinau tomorrow?" Charlotte suggested. I agreed.

"I wonder if they have a decent restaurant," Charlotte mumbled. I asked the woman at the reception desk for a room.

"Impossible," she replied. "It's not safe here. You might be shot."

"Shot?"

"The front line is just over there," she said and pointed at the Dniester River.

"There's actual fighting now?"

"Yes, snipers fire across the river."

"It seems perfectly safe to me," Charlotte said. We both suspected the receptionist was exaggerating but she insisted that we sleep at a different hotel a few blocks back from the river. We picked up our bags and walked to the next hotel.

"Cossacks," Charlotte said, as we stood by the check-in desk. I turned and saw mismatched uniforms.

"Just our luck," Charlotte added. "Trapped in a hotel with fifty drunk Cossacks." After dark, we went down to the restaurant for dinner, but the door was locked. A sign said Closed for Curfew. We banged on the door. When a waiter arrived, he agreed to sell us bread and cheese for dollars. We ate this small picnic on our saggy hotel beds, then went to sleep.

"Wake up." I felt Charlotte shake my shoulder. "Did you hear that?" I listened for a minute, then heard the pop of a gun, less distinctive than Grozny gunfire, but someone was shooting.

"We need to take cover," Charlotte said. She slid under the bed. I felt no adrenaline rush.

"Come on," Charlotte urged. I crawled under my bed.

"Snipers?" Charlotte asked.

"Who knows," I said. "It might just be some Cossack celebration."

"Those shots came from the direction of the river. They're fighting," Charlotte insisted. We waited until the gunfire stopped and then climbed back into our beds, Charlotte's white nightgown now speckled with dust. The gunfire started again. We slid under the beds. Once it was quiet again, we got back into them. After an hour of this, we both gave up and stayed in bed.

Charlotte woke first in the morning.

"Come on. Let's get out of here," she said. We packed our bags, paid the bill and stood outside the hotel. We flagged down cars.

"Chisinau?" the first driver snorted. "I'd never make it there alive." We stood on the street for nearly an hour but could not find a driver who would take us.

"You don't think we're stuck here do you?" Charlotte asked. We returned to the hotel reception desk and asked to check back in.

"Why, you just checked out?" the receptionist said. When she heard our story, she said "Of course. No one will go to Moldova. It's dangerous." Go to Moldova? We are in Moldova, I thought, but kept quiet. I still wanted a room. Pointing out that no government recognized Transdniestrian independence might mean eviction.

"But you don't understand," Charlotte said. "I have to cross for a London flight. I'll lose my ticket and I can't afford another. I'll miss my exams. This is academic D-day. These are my final exams. My degree's at stake." The receptionist shrugged her shoulders and handed us a key.

After we had checked back in, we heard about funeral services in the main square for Cossacks who had been killed and decided to attend. We left the hotel and walked toward the square.

"Bizarre," Charlotte said as a military vehicle – an armoured car, I guessed – passed by. It looked like a fortified garden shed on wheels.

"That must be home made," I said. I felt worried by this escalation. We had only seen guns before.

"I think they're gearing up for a fight. Why don't you come back to Kiev and catch a flight from there?" I suggested to Charlotte.

"I can't." Like a homing pigeon, Charlotte remained determined to find a way over the river, through Moldova and back to Romania.

In the square, people stood by open coffins. We saw two. The bodies of young men lay inside. Men with megaphones chanted anti-Moldovan slogans. One shouted that changes in the alphabet from Cyrillic to Roman letters would be the first step by the Moldovan government to merge Moldova with Romania. An elderly woman came up to Charlotte and me. She said, "How can I learn a new alphabet at my age?" I sympathized but thought there must be a better way to resolve such conflict than with guns.

The next day passed slowly. We went to see the general in charge of Russian forces based in Trans-Dniester. General Lebed was a giant of a man. I shook his hand and guessed it must be three times the size of mine. We tried to extract information on how Russian forces planned to respond to the escalating conflict. Charlotte also explained her predicament of not being able find a way over to the Chisinau side. General Lebed joked that he planned to attack the next day and that we could have a lift over in his tank.

With so much time on our hands, we'd even become friendly with the Cossacks in our hotel. We spent the evening with them. They played their guitars and sang songs for us. Their words became increasingly slurred as they tanked up on moonshine.

The next morning, we visited government offices, hopeful there might now be an open route across the Dniester River so that we could reach Chisinau. As we approached one building, a bus pulled up alongside it. A Cossack who stood near us said the bus would travel to Dubasari. We knew that a bridge there crossed the Dniester, but no one knew if this bridge remained open. The Cossack boarded the bus. We followed.

Women sat in some of the front seats. We moved down the aisle to empty seats near the back. Once we had settled in and looked around, we realized that all the other passengers were Cossacks.

"They're armed!" Charlotte said. "Should we get off?" I hesitated. A broad woman, who was at least six feet tall, came on to the bus. She stood by the driver in her fur coat, the fibres long and matted in spots. The engine idled, the door remained open.

This woman held a large gold crucifix. She raised her arms and blessed the bus.

"The Don Cossack mother," a Cossack who sat nearby told us. Mother left the bus. The door slammed shut and we rumbled down the road.

"Susan, should we ask to get off?" Charlotte said, more insistent now. I hesitated again and then walked to the front of the bus.

"Please stop and let us off," I said to the driver.

"It's dangerous. I can't," he replied. "Get back, stay out of sight." As I turned to walk back, I saw that a Cossack was now sitting in my seat. He flirted with Charlotte. He leaned forward and showed her something that I could not yet see. He moved when I came back.

"Bloody hell," Charlotte said. "They have grenades." I looked and saw the Cossack holding one in his hand, a small green metal pineapple with a pin on top. He rolled it across his palm. Then he threw the grenade, like a baseball, over our heads. His friends joined in this game of catch. Charlotte and I watched in terror. How long could it possibly be before a Cossack missed, the grenade crashed to the floor, the pin dislodged and then, kaboom.

Mikhail came back and told the men to put the grenade away and pull the bus curtains shut. Most had done so long ago.

"Moldovan snipers fire along these banks," Mikhail said. "You girls will be much safer if you sit down there." Charlotte and I slid off our seats onto the floor, where he pointed. Someone gave us rolls of white bandages and said, "In case you're hit." We sat eye level with Cossack knees and held our bandages. Common sense now returned to me. I felt ashamed at the lack of it earlier and that I willingly remained on this bus ride for crazy people.

"They can't shoot at journalists," Charlotte said. "We should make signs." With a plan, no matter how unrealistic, we felt in control again. We dug into our bags for pens and paper and made signs that said Press in English, French and Russian.

Charlotte stood up to affix the signs on the bus windows with bandage tape. The Cossacks ordered her down. I felt the bus lurch sharply right, away from the river. The Cossacks parted the curtains a few inches and peered out. Then they pulled the curtains wide open. I saw treetops and blue sky. We had pulled back from the river front line.

Mikhail came back for a visit. "We'll be at the headquarters in five minutes," he said.

When we arrived, we went inside and learned that the bridge was closed. There was no route to cross over here. Discouraged, we asked about transport back to Tiraspol. Mikhail volunteered to help us find a ride. We followed him out of the headquarters and onto a nearby road. He stood in the middle of it, with a Kalashnikov hanging from his shoulder. Cars stopped, but not for long.

"He looks threatening with his Kalashnikov, but he's far too polite to use it," Charlotte said. "Just look at that. He's asking all those drivers if they'll give us a lift. They say no and then he just says okay then!" Eventually we gave up and went back to the headquarters. As we approached, we saw a taxi parked outside. We asked the driver if he knew a safe road to Tiraspol.

"The back highway is open," he said

"There's an interior road that doesn't face the river?" I asked. He shrugged and said, "Of course." I was angry at the Cossacks and now realized that ride had been a test. The Cossacks wanted to show they could drive along the front line, that they still controlled this side. We had taken an unnecessary risk. I still felt ashamed that I did not get us off the bus as Charlotte suggested. We negotiated a fare with the taxi driver for Tiraspol and drove back in silence.

When we reached the hotel, we bumped into a Japanese camera crew. The cameraman knew a route over the river. The crew had a Jeep and offered Charlotte a lift. We parted company. I headed back to my side in Kiev. Charlotte would soon leave for hers. The Cossacks stayed in Trans-Dniester, defending what they considered was Slav land from the Moldovans.

Such turf battles extended to business, and this is what now occupied me in Ukraine. State companies were being privatized. I spent most of May investigating deals and trying to understand the complicated transactions occurring over who would control key infrastructure like pipelines that carried gas from Russia through Ukraine to Europe. I had no time to track anything else, so I was caught off guard by a battle in the Transdniestrian town Bendery in June. I decided to take a break from investigating business deals so that I could go to Bendery.

When I reached Bendery, the fighting was over. About three hundred people, including civilians, had been killed. The sun shone brightly. Russian troops had secured a buffer zone. People who lived in no man's land wandered around. They looked for bottled water, lined up to buy bread and gossiped about the latest events. Tanks were scattered around their neighbourhood with hatches opened. Soldiers squatted or sat on the ground nearby. Everyone looked relaxed. I spoke to many people who had been present during the battle. None was hurt or lost family members or friends.

As I chatted with one man, soldiers in the distance threw sacks onto an open-back truck. The sacks looked odd but so did the entire neighbourhood. The man said, "Such a pity," and pointed at the truck. I looked and focused my attention. Then

I realized the soldiers loaded dead bodies onto the truck. The bodies lay stacked in neat rows. I could not believe this conflict between "us" and "them" had become so lethal. I stared at a truck full of bagged corpses and felt nothing. I saw tanks and guns and soldiers; spent cartridges littered the ground. These empty shells may have housed bullets that killed some of those people. I picked up one of the brass cartridges and put it in my pocket. Maybe if I looked at it later I would respond properly to these horrifying events. For now, none of this seemed real.

9

SHOPPING AND A CIVIL WAR

"This doesn't look good," I warned Charlotte. We stood at the Aeroflot desk in Boryspil airport.

"Your flight's delayed," the attendant said.

"For how long?" I asked.

"Who knows?" she replied. "Yesterday no flights took off – no fuel." Charlotte and I shuffled back to our seats in the departure lounge.

"How can she not know when the plane will take off?" Charlotte asked. She had arrived back in Kiev in September, a month earlier, and decided to join me on this trip. It would be my last before leaving Kiev to begin a new job in London at the BBC. The *Financial Times* had commissioned Charlotte to write a piece about shopping in Central Asia. I was on holiday, but planned to use the trip to build contacts that would be useful for my London job.

"It's been bad since independence but never quite this bad. Russia's selling Ukraine a lot less fuel now. Corruption doesn't help. One official here sold a shipment for Ukraine's air force on the black market."

"And pocketed the proceeds?" Charlotte guessed. I nodded. "The pilots didn't have any fuel to fly, so they spent their time playing soccer on the runways." We chatted about what we would do when we landed in Tashkent and reminisced about our last Central Asian shopping spree.

"I turned all that silk into seat covers," Charlotte said. I envied her domestic skills. I had copied her and staggered out with bag loads of silk from that musty Tashkent market store, but most of the silk sat untouched in my cupboard.

"I don't usually like shopping, but I've become an addict. I think it's all those years living under Communism with nothing but bare shop shelves," I told her. I was worried about the ongoing delay, so I went back to the counter to check on our flight status.

The woman at the information desk suggested that we fly to the Kyrgyz capital, Bishkek, instead of Tashkent.

"How far is Bishkek from Tashkent?"

"Nearly six hundred kilometres."

"The road conditions?"

"Girl, I work for an airline, how should I know?" She had a point. After so many journeys on potholed roads that disappeared into ruts I felt skeptical about the possibility of a decent connection between these capitals. Still, Bishkek, the site of a political meeting, did eventually feature on our itinerary and the Aeroflot woman seemed confident that the Bishkek flight, scheduled to take off at 1:15 p.m., would fly. The tickets cost the equivalent of a few dollars each so that even on our limited budgets we could afford to buy tickets for that flight and for every other flight leaving for any Central Asian destination over the next few days.

Someone's information was not very good. At check-in that afternoon, the Aeroflot woman said, with no hint of an apology, "that flight is cancelled. The only one leaving before 8 p.m. is the flight to Leningrad." Defeated, we gave up and went home. A pizza delivery service had recently opened in Kiev. I thought that fresh pizza would be some consolation for a wasted day with no food at the airport.

I dialed the number for Vezuvia. The woman who answered told me to pick up the pizza myself.

"But you're meant to deliver."

"The driver's away and we don't know when he'll come back."

"Could you take my number and call me when he does?" The woman agreed. It wasn't an entirely hopeless situation because she also took our order, which meant that the chef must be there.

Charlotte and I stacked our plane tickets on the kitchen table and then went through them to figure out which flight would leave next.

"I'd better call the Aeroflot office for an update on the fuel situation," I said to Charlotte. My finger became sore from dialing a line that was constantly busy. After half an hour, someone finally answered. The woman on the other end said that the flight for Bishkek had been rescheduled and would fly but that the tickets we held would no longer be valid.

Before I could reserve new tickets, the woman put the phone handset on the counter. At least she did not hang up. I heard her complaining to a co-worker about the high cost of bus tickets. I shouted and whistled down the phone to catch her attention, but I think that she disliked work and therefore ignored me. After ten minutes, I decided that she would never return, so I hung up.

The phone then rang. It was the Vezuvia lady. She said that the driver had arrived and would deliver our order. Within twenty minutes a large cheese, tomato and pepperoni pizza sat on the table. Charlotte tried to figure out how to fit it into the oven but was interrupted by the ringing of the doorbell. She opened the door. My landlord stood there, surprised to find us home. I understood that we interfered with his plans.

When I first rented the apartment a year and a half earlier, I returned home from a trip late one night. I heard laughter from the kitchen as I unlocked my apartment door and pushed it open. I glanced down at my watch – it was past midnight. I dragged my bag over the threshold and left it in the hallway by a large bookcase. Then I stood and listened. I recognized my landlord's voice. Why was he here? Who were those other people with him? I was tired and wanted to go to bed. But it seemed that night that I had one more issue to settle before I crawled into bed.

I walked through the small vestibule, around a corner and down the long hallway that led past a galley kitchen to the dining area. My landlord and three of his friends were sitting at the table. The vodka long gone, they were now sobering up with coffee. A few empty cups stood scattered across the table.

"Susan! You're home! We didn't expect you," my landlord said.

Didn't expect me? I was so tired that I could not even search for the correct words in Russian to ask him what he was doing here. Why had he moved in and thrown a party while I was away? Renting an apartment had only become possible once I received accreditation. Locals rarely rented and with so few foreigners in Kiev, few people here had experience as landlords. My landlord and I were still negotiating the terms of the landlord-tenant relationship. I thought we'd made progress but realized now that we still had some way to go.

As I stood there, one of my landlord's friends asked for a drink. My landlord said, "Susan, you're the hostess, make some more coffee." I glared at him. Realizing they had overstayed their welcome, they packed up and left.

Tonight, I saw that my landlord held a bag with a large watermelon. He came into the kitchen and cut pieces for us. He chatted for a few minutes, said that if a man or a woman phoned for him that I should tell them to meet him at the cinema next door. Then he left. At 9 p.m. my landlord arrived back at the apartment with his boss and a woman. We passed in the hallway of our building. Charlotte and I were returning to the airport, hoping to get on the Bishkek flight. (Work on the landlord-tenant relationship would have to wait.)

Now the woman at the Aeroflot desk (did she never go home?) insisted that we register for a flight to the Turkmen capital, Ashgabat, instead of Bishkek. I knew that Ashgabat was 1,300 kilometres from Tashkent, the city that we eventually hoped to reach, but at this point I thought that anywhere in Central Asia would do. Charlotte understood the conversation. She stood erect, eyes opened wide. She shouted, "I can't believe it." She walked quickly through the waiting area and shouted, "I can't believe it" over and over again. The Aeroflot woman sympathized. *"Nervnyi stress* [nervous stress]*,"* she said and handed us two boarding passes for the flight to Ashgabat.

We landed at 7 a.m. I had no visa for Ashgabat; I never even wanted to be here. Independent now, Turkmenistan should have customs and passport control, but no one asked us any questions. We walked out of the airport without a document check and took a taxi to a hotel.

"One double room please," I said to the receptionist.

"Do you have a reservation?"

"No, may I make one now?"

"Reservations must be made in advance."

"But you have empty rooms." Silence. I begged. She refused.

I longed for capitalism where reservations depended only on vacancy rates and the ability to pay. We tried other hotels. The receptionist at the Jubilee, which housed the American embassy, said no, as did the receptionist at the Tourist. We did not mind being rejected there quite as much because we noticed that parts of the lobby ceiling had collapsed. The stairs also seemed unstable. The Tourist receptionist sent us to the Ashgabat Hotel but warned us that that it would be impossible for us to check in there; she was right.

Under the circumstances a small lie seemed acceptable. Back at the Tourist desk, I told the receptionist that the Ukrainian diplomatic service had forwarded a reservation booking for us and that the hotel must have misplaced it. The receptionist lied right back.

"We have no rooms," she said. (The hotel was so empty that our footsteps echoed in the lobby.) "Besides the Tourist doesn't take foreign guests, so the telegram shouldn't have been sent here in the first place." The receptionist seemed mildly interested in our case. We decided that we would camp out in the lobby and not leave until she gave us a room.

A few hours later, someone in the hotel chain of authority agreed to check us in. The hotel receptionist, now a friend and an ally, led us through deserted hallways to our room. When we entered and flicked on the light, I saw a cockroach scuttle under the bathroom door.

"Girls, we have other guests, sheiks from Kuwait," the receptionist said. We learned that a large group of about thirty sheiks had come to Turkmenistan on a hunting trip. The sheiks were travelling with their own falcons.

"Could we meet them?" Charlotte asked. The receptionist gestured that we should follow. She led us down the hallway to a door that she opened without even knocking.

A Kuwaiti bird tender in white cotton pyjamas lay on a bed in the room, asleep. Three falcons, hooded but seemingly alert, stood on a makeshift cylindrical perch, a rolled-up blanket wrapped tightly with packing tape. The receptionist, who was not shy, bent down and squeezed the bird tender's feet. He woke up and seemed surprised but good-natured. He smiled and offered to show us the birds, clearly proud of the three falcons in his care.

He put on a thick leather glove, which was long enough to cover part of his forearm, and then removed the hood from one of the falcons. It screeched, stretched its wings and hopped onto his gloved hand. The falcon settled down quickly and peered around with an intense look in its eyes. It was tethered, like the others, so that it could not fly around.

"Where are the sheiks?" Charlotte asked. "Could we meet them?" The receptionist took us down to the second-floor lobby. The sheiks sat cross-legged in a circle on the floor. They wore long white desert robes with red checked scarves tied around their heads. One sheik spoke English. He told us that he and his friends would soon leave for the Turkmen mountains, where they would camp for twenty days. He offered to take us with them. We thanked them but said we would not be staying for long. The sheik who spoke English said that he and his friends usually hunted in Iraq but could no longer go there (we assumed, because of conflict), so they had come to Turkmenistan instead.

The hunting trip seemed extravagant. The sheiks had rented two jets – one for the men and their birds, and the second for Jeeps. I thought the sheiks were probably also extravagant shoppers. We could not confirm this; the hotel receptionist told us that we just missed the weekly Ashgabat market. I felt disappointed but resigned to missing out on a trip to the market. I did not want to stay six more days in Ashgabat. Shopping would have to wait.

We returned to the American embassy, which was located at the Jubilee Hotel, for interviews. I already imagined myself hard at work in London, with a hotline to the ambassador in Turkmenistan, if news ever broke out there. The makeshift embassy occupied half a dozen rooms. A wardrobe marked the entrance. Placed sideways, it jutted across half the corridor. A large circular plaque with an American eagle on it hung from a nail driven into the wardrobe. When someone bumped it, the plaque swayed and wobbled. So far it had not fallen off. Once "inside" the embassy, the territory was secure as most of the doors were fitted with elaborate locks.

Only four countries – the U.S., Iran, China and Pakistan – had embassies in Ashgabat. The Americans shared their hotel floor with the Iranians. Strained relations between the two countries meant the Americans were not allowed to talk to their Iranian neighbours. It must have been a lonely life at this U.S. outpost in Turkmenistan. I looked forward to leaving.

Roland, a political secretary, briefed us. He knew the region well and talked for a long time. He seemed depressed. I sympathized, having experienced near complete isolation during my early days in Kiev. Charlotte invited Roland to join us for dinner that night.

An impressive collection of Turkmen carpets lay heaped in a colourful pile by Roland's colleague's desk. I eyed the carpets enviously and wanted to ask if I could buy one.

After wrapping up our interviews, we inquired about getting tickets to Tashkent at the Aeroflot office but faced the usual grim news. No planes had fuel. None would fly. When would someone rebel? A vast hydrocarbon reservoir, this whole region still shipped all of its fuel to Moscow.

Stuck in Ashgabat, not even able to shop, we read the Lonely Planet guide for suggestions about what places to visit. It recommended an underwater thermal lake at mountains near the Iranian border, about an hour's drive away. Our hotel receptionist, now quite helpful, also told us about the lake. She said that Intourist ran guided swims there. We decided we wanted to visit the lake, so she booked a car to take us there.

We drove through flat, scrubby terrain. We saw a herd of camels on one side and a ridge of mountains on the other. Eventually we reached an inconspicuous left turning. A small, wooden complex stood at the end of the drive. A burly Intourist guide emerged from inside. We paid him and he led us toward the mouth of a cave in an outcropping of rock.

Spotlights angled toward the craggy roof cast rough, angular shadows. We followed the guide down a steep staircase that turned. We could not see the lake below but felt the temperature rise as we descended.

After a long climb down we reached a flat area with two metal sheds that smelled. These changing rooms must have doubled as lavatories. As we put on our bathing suits, we were careful not to step off the wooden planks onto the suspiciously moist earthen floor.

"You won't need that," the Turkmen guide said. He pointed at a raincoat that Charlotte wore. "Or that," he added and tugged the towel I had wrapped around myself. I followed Charlotte as we descended the final flight of stairs to the lake. She turned for a moment and stared up at me with large, doleful eyes. Our guide stood in front of Charlotte. He wore a tight swimsuit that left the top part of his buttocks exposed in an unattractive way.

We slid into the dark lake.

"It's lovely and warm, a lot like a hot bath," Charlotte said. The guide paddled nearby. He held a life preserver ring and wore flippers on his feet. Charlotte and I both swam out, doing the breaststroke.

"I don't think he knows how to swim," Charlotte said. She gestured at the guide, who clutched the life preserver.

"Take hold girls, take hold," he said. Charlotte grabbed the opposite side of the life preserver. I swam alone, a little behind. The guide led us out of the light, toward the back of the cave, where he promised to stop at a crag for a rest.

"But we're not tired," I said. Soon we stood on a rock ledge, perched against the cave wall.

"Oi!" Charlotte screamed. "Stop that! He groped me!" I shouted too as the guide squeezed my waist and then the side of my breast. No matter how loudly we screamed, down here, no one would hear us. If he wanted to, this guide could drown us and dismiss it all as an unfortunate accident.

Charlotte insisted that he take us back. I translated. The guide agreed. We had no choice but to follow as we were disoriented in the dark. I heard Charlotte beside me but could not see her. We clutched the life preserver and allowed the guide to drag us through the water.

Charlotte put the relationship back on civil footing with polite chit-chat. I welcomed the opportunity to translate and occupy my mind with something other than thoughts of revenge.

"Have you ever seen a fish in this lake?" Charlotte asked the guide. I saw a dim light, so I knew that the guide had not tricked us; shore lay ahead.

When we arrived, we ran and pulled on the locked changing room door. The guide had the key. We waited for him.

"You can change here, with me," he said. "I want to see you naked."

"No bloody way!" Charlotte shouted. She was so adamant that he backed off and opened the door. It was quiet at first inside the changing room. But we soon heard loud bangs as the guide's feet struck the metal walls.

"He's breaking in," I said.

"There's not much of a roof. I think he's climbing up so that he can see us change from the top," Charlotte replied. All this from a state employee at a state-run tourist site; so much for local charm.

It suddenly became quiet. We suspected this was because the guide had found a chink in the metal sheets and was watching us. We dressed underneath our towels. Then we opened the door and ran up the stairs. They were steep and the guide, quick. He shot ahead of me and ran behind Charlotte. I could see him pinch her bottom. He fell back behind me and pinched my bottom. Then, with a burst of energy, he repositioned himself between us again.

We all stopped to catch our breath. The guide insisted that he carry my bag, an act considered both polite and manly in this part of the world. When I refused, he grabbed it from me. Charlotte and I ran. He followed and pinched our bottoms all the way to the top.

Charlotte arrived there first. She turned around and shouted that she wanted to kick the guard in the balls but that she worried he might fall down backwards and break his neck or land on me.

Charlotte screamed at him in English. Out of breath, in a quiet fury, I translated. "I want to give him a piece of my mind," she shouted. "Tell him you can't treat women like that. How would he feel if someone did this to his sisters?" The guide looked bemused. From his expression, we knew that no sister of his would ever dream of swimming with a strange man in an underground lake.

Fortunately our driver was still waiting for us. We told him what had happened. He laughed, and then saw a good opportunity. He insisted on twice the fare we had initially agreed upon before he would take us to Ashgabat. We reluctantly paid him the fare he demanded because we wanted to get away.

We arrived back in time for dinner with Roland. He suggested going out for "pizza, of a sort." We could choose a puffy dough ball with unidentifiable meat or a puffy dough ball with a splash of ketchup. Roland suggested the meatless version would be safer.

"This is the 135th time I've had dinner at this restaurant," he said. "Six months down and a year and a half to go."

I left the table to use the bathroom. When I arrived back, Roland briefly excused himself.

"He's very sad," Charlotte told me. "He used to live in Africa where he saw giraffes all the time. He said he'd made the terrible mistake of studying Russian and when the Soviet Union collapsed, the State Department urgently rounded up all its Russian speakers and posted him here."

When we arrived back at the hotel, the receptionist had good news: the woman from Aeroflot had called to offer us tickets on a Bishkek flight that would depart at 4 a.m. We tried to sleep for a few hours, but Montezuma's revenge kept us up, fighting for the bathroom.

On the way to the airport, Charlotte said that earlier in the week she'd dreamed we would cross Central Asia in a propeller plane. I told her that the distances were too vast for this. When we arrived at the terminal, the ticket agent shook her head — no need for explanation. We already understood the Bishkek flight was cancelled. The agent suggested that we wait, just in case.

We stretched out on the sofas. The Aeroflot woman later shook us from deep sleep — the captain had found fuel, so the flight would leave. We walked onto the tarmac in hazy early morning light. One propeller plane stood parked on the runway. Our flight would take seven and a half hours.

We boarded and sat in our seats. Suspicious of Aeroflot flights and worried about fuel shortages, Charlotte made the sign of the cross and asked, "What if we run out of fuel and crash in mid-air?" Tired, I fastened my seat belt and fell asleep. I woke when Charlotte poked me. When I opened my eyes, I noticed an orangey reflection in the window.

"Did you see that?" she asked. "A flame just shot out of the engine. I think you should tell someone." I shuffled to the back of the plane and reported the incident to the flight attendant. She shrugged her shoulders and said, "It happens all the time."

We landed in Bishkek hours before a scheduled meeting of leaders from all over the region to discuss trade and other economic matters. This was the first time since we had left Kiev that we managed to reach an intended destination on time. As the only foreign reporters present, we had unlimited access for interviews and even though I was technically on holiday, not at work, I considered this a journalistic triumph. The information would be useful for feature stories that I could write later.

Kiosks at the meeting site displayed local goods but sold none. Charlotte admired tall white felt Kyrgyz hats with black velvet trim. "They're just like fairy princess hats," she said. "I'd like to buy some." We investigated and soon learned the name of the factory that made the hats. When the meeting finished, we left for the factory.

The guard at the gate had gone; the entrance stood deserted. We walked in and climbed the central staircase. We heard the steady clatter of sewing machines; the women who operated them filled a large room. Pleased, even excited, by overseas visitors they took our orders and asked us to return the next day for the hats.

Next we visited the American embassy. The ambassador, an intelligent and kind man, briefed us on local politics. He also spoke at length and enthusiastically about mountain climbing. He recommended that we visit the Tien Shan range. I told him about my trip into these mountains on the Chinese side a few months earlier. I travelled with a group of Hong Kong tourists whom I'd met in Urumqi. A sheep had been slaughtered for a barbecue dinner held in our honour. Later, the Hong Kong tourists and I spent a night in a yurt. I remembered the still mountain air and silt green lakes and told the ambassador about a horse ride at dawn. I sat on a sturdy local horse, behind my guide. The horse carried us down steep cliffs. All we heard was the sound of birds and the trickle of a mountain stream.

"Let's go into the mountains near here," Charlotte said. We did not venture high. We remained in a forested alpine landscape filled with icy streams. Charlotte stripped down for a dip. She dreamed of a swim in the Oxus (Amu Darya) River, but said this would do for now. We enjoyed our brief, hassle-free stay in Kyrgyzstan so much that we felt certain our luck had changed and the rest of our trip would proceed smoothly.

After our hike in the mountains, we returned to Bishkek. We went to the Aeroflot office to buy tickets to our next destination, which was Tashkent. An efficient agent served us. She sold us the tickets and never mentioned a word about fuel.

We saw colleagues from London at the Tashkent airport. One lived in the city. He invited us to stay. Not wanting to impose, we said that we would find a hotel. Our colleague looked worried and insisted that we write down his address and contact number.

No hotel would check us in. A man followed us everywhere we went. One receptionist whispered that we had "a friend." A security services agent had appeared once before. When I landed in Almaty, Kazakhstan, on my way back from China a tall, personable, fit man took my suitcases at the airport, flagged down a car and asked whether two hundred roubles was an acceptable fare. I agreed. He told the taxi driver to take me to a hotel in the centre. I thanked him and boarded the taxi.

"Do you work for the KGB like your friend?" the driver asked. Offended, I asked what he meant, especially as the KGB did not even exist anymore and its Russian successor technically should not function in an independent Uzbekistan.

"He showed me his identity card – he's from the KGB." KGB or not, I appreciated the hotel tip. Boris Manço, a Turkish pop star, was staying there. I bumped into his brother in the elevator and he invited me to join them for dinner. Saudis flooded the region with religious books and money. Turks mounted a cultural charm offensive. They forged ties through music.

Charlotte and I hoped that this security agent would prove equally helpful and direct a receptionist to check us in. He did not. His presence sabotaged all possibility of accommodation. Everyone seemed afraid.

After several hours, we gave up. Fortunately we had our colleague's address. When we rang the doorbell, he did not look surprised to see us. He already had beds made up. He told us that the political climate in Uzbekistan had deteriorated since our springtime visit; the country had slid into authoritarian rule. The next day we confirmed this through interviews with leaders from government and opposition parties. Then we shopped.

Neither of us wanted to leave the market, but soon we could carry no more merchandise. Shopping bags did not exist in this part of the world. Vendors helped us find sacks. Between us we carted away twenty-four glazed earthenware dinner plates, two full Uzbek tea sets, one medium-sized Bukhara rug and two silk wedding gowns that resembled those on display in a museum (fortunately not pilfered). When we visited local museums, the cashiers offered us items that may well have come straight from the display cases.

One country remained on our travel itinerary – Tajikistan. It bordered Uzbekistan. In the spring we crossed with ease; now, every visit to the Aeroflot office was an exercise in frustration. I could not purchase one ticket for any of the multiple destinations on the Tajik side of the border. We assumed no tickets meant more fuel shortages. After several trips, we succeeded and bought tickets for a tiny border town flight later that week. The Aeroflot agent also offered us cheap tickets for the next day to the Uzbek tourist town Khiva. An urban jewel on UNESCO's World Heritage Sites list, Khiva seemed as good an interim destination as any.

We had not yet learned one simple lesson. Travelling in an authoritarian regime is hell. In the departure lounge at Tashkent airport, we met a Canadian couple from Moscow. They were pale and had bags under their eyes and wrinkled clothing. They had been stuck there for two days. The deflated young man and his wilted blonde partner had planned a romantic getaway to Khiva, but the airport guards would not allow them to board any flight, even though they had valid visas and airline tickets. Bewildered, they gave up and returned to Moscow.

Sure enough, the guards also refused us permission to board our flight and offered no explanation. A six-hour showdown began. Then the guards changed their minds and allowed us onto a flight. I had no energy left to even ask them why. We buckled ourselves into our seats, fully expecting the guards to change their minds again and drag us off.

We landed, but faced another battle at the hotel. Charlotte saved the day. After we had spent hours pleading with the receptionist to check us in Charlotte threw her arms back and let out a howl. Compassionate after all, the receptionist ran to put the kettle on and made us tea. Then she found us a room on a deserted floor.

"A British documentary filmmaker is staying in this room but he's away for a few days," the receptionist told us.

"Which filmmaker?" Charlotte asked.

"Michael Palin," the receptionist said.

Khiva, beautiful in that arid, dusty, Central Asian way, is a city museum and therefore pristinely maintained. An ornery camel stood tethered by a small ladder, fitted with a saddle blanket, a puffy cushion and a large stick, presumably there to help passengers maintain control. Colourful minarets and domes jutted up from an otherwise sand-baked beige cityscape. The usual cauldron of plov (a rice and meat dish) simmered away outside one café. Khiva lacked tourists; I blamed the guards at Tashkent airport for this. But we enjoyed the peace, at least until we visited the city walls, which were one of Khiva's historic sites.

We purchased our entrance tickets for the walls, climbed up and admired the view from the top. Soon a group of children circled us. They ranged in age from about six to fourteen years old. We stood in the middle; the children surrounded us. We understood from preliminary chit-chat that these were not curious youngsters interested in meeting foreigners; their motives seemed more malign. As we stood there, Charlotte and I debated what to do.

"We can't possibly hit them," Charlotte said. "They're just children" Perhaps a security guard might appear. Or, we could wait until the children grew bored and drifted away. After a while, we realized this would not happen. The children enjoyed trapping us like prey.

"Should I swear at them?" We agreed that I should try. I only knew one expletive in Russian, which was an insult to mothers. As soon as I said it, I realized I had made a mistake and that I had probably uttered the worst possible insult. In retaliation, the children attacked us, their small hands and legs lashing out in fury. The boys seemed most interested in pinching our bottoms and breasts. One tried to take our bags. We were scared and managed to break through the circle and ran for the stairs, still receiving the odd slap along the way from children positioned nearby. A few of them tried to push Charlotte down the stairs.

Once off the wall, we found the premises security guard and reported the children. "Sometimes they're there," he said. "Sometimes they aren't." That was it. I wondered if he ran the gang. Once again we had paid for a ticket to a state-run tourist site ticket only to face assault.

One other Uzbek museum visit was nearly just as bad. Much Soviet nuclear testing took place in Central Asia. We accidentally wandered into a museum of mutants. We saw a multi-legged chicken and ran out screaming. The woman in charge came after us shouting "Wait, wait, you haven't seen our sheep."

Even during doomed trips, moments occur when all goes to plan. Our plane reached Tashkent on time. Our shopping remained in our colleague's apartment. Charlotte, who had spent the summer reporting from Bosnia for the *Daily Mail*, had experience in a war zone and understood the importance of travelling light. She suggested that we leave our shopping behind and collect it on our way back from Tajikistan.

I felt shocked, even betrayed by this suggestion. I did not want to be separated from my shopping. In some way this crockery that had cost pennies, weighed a ton and might be decorated with poisonous lead paint represented my future life. I had decorated the living room of the house that I did not yet own with the carpet, hats and gowns. I looked forward to serving my friends meals on Central Asian plates and to brewing tea in the Tashkent pot.

I tried logic. "Based on our experience with flights so far, if we leave the shopping behind, we might never see it again." Charlotte, a non-Communist country resident and therefore less shopping deprived than I was, retained her common sense. We argued back and forth over the merits of travelling light versus laden down with the contents of an entire household. I won, probably only because I rarely fought and so my passion on this subject must have seemed unusual enough to indulge.

Our flight took off as scheduled. We travelled with our usual luggage and our sacks of shopping. When we landed I realized, to my surprise, that although we had arrived near the Uzbek-Tajik border we remained in Uzbekistan. Even though I had studied a local map to match what Aeroflot tickets were available with an appropriate Tajik destination, I had made a mistake. I blamed this on poor quality paper and ink. The dot that marked our destination on the map was smudged, appearing to be in Tajikistan, but we were not.

We took a taxi to the border. The driver said that he could not cross, so we would have to walk into Tajikistan. Others did the same. A group of men carried our bags and all of our shopping. They showed us the bus bound for the Tajik capital, Dushanbe. A short bumpy ride later we arrived there. The hotel receptionist gave us a room with no fuss, even without a reservation. Intourist check-in rules remained a mystery. The receptionist told us that another journalist had arrived earlier and gave us his name and room number.

It took time to contact our colleague. We left a note inviting him to meet us for dinner. He did not respond. Eventually we bumped into him in the lobby. He said he had assumed that prostitutes had written the note, so he did not reply. He told us about reports of unrest in southern Tajikistan, near the Afghan border. An Islamic-democratic coalition currently held power. Reports said that the Russian army backed a pro-Communist tribal alliance to challenge the government. Nothing had happened yet, but we thought that we should travel south and investigate.

We approached taxi drivers in the market. No driver would make the trip. I felt uneasy after the Tiraspol experience.

One driver whom we approached suggested that we try a market vendor who sold car parts. The driver said this man had an apartment in a southern city called Qurgonteppa, not far from the Afghan border. We found the man and introduced ourselves. He immediately agreed to drive us to Qurgonteppa.

"There's been some fighting there," he said. "I'd like to see my apartment and make sure that it wasn't damaged." Relatives had told the man that the fighting had stopped.

The next morning, the driver met us at our hotel. A narrow ribbon of road comprised the main highway south. At first we encountered traffic typical of rural life. Men on bicycles drove a flock of sheep down the road. The sheep stretched across both lanes and moved slowly, so we inched along behind the flock until a shepherd guided it onto scrubby pasture land. For a while the traffic flowed well. We travelled behind boxy Ladas and trucks loaded with agricultural produce. Any scavenger who followed the trucks could assemble a good dinner of vegetables, grain or the odd chicken that fell off the backs.

Then things began to look not so normal. We passed a tractor pulled over on the opposite side of the road. We thought that a large gas canister on the tractor hood signified that the driver needed gas. His tractor pulled a trailer with walls made of mesh metal that was filled with children and bundles of clothes, instead of the usual load of cotton. We did not immediately register the significance. We continued down the highway.

Soon we saw a motorcycle on the opposite side of the road. A dozen passengers clung to a sidecar meant to carry one. No one would travel any significant distance like this for fun. Next came another tractor, with two cotton trailers hitched behind like a mini-train. Once again children, bundles and a few women filled the trailers – the driver was the only man on board. More and more passenger-laden agricultural vehicles that should have been used for the harvest inched up the road. I recorded two hundred. Then I stopped counting the exodus of refugees.

About three kilometres from Qurgonteppa, a truck driver who ferried women and children crammed in the open back flashed his lights at us. The truck had stopped on the other side of the road. Our taxi driver pulled over. Charlotte and I crossed the road and approached the truck. We could not understand what the women were saying. Some cried and many spoke at once. Eventually I thought they told us that tanks had just opened fire in Qurgonteppa and that some of their children had been killed. As the truck drove away, the women shouted, "Run, the tanks are coming."

Despite having bad knees, we both sprinted back to the taxi and told the driver what we had learned. He did a sharp U-turn and raced up the road toward Dushanbe. In the backseat, I said to Charlotte, "But we haven't really seen anything for ourselves. We didn't actually see the tanks." We noticed a small guard-house by the side of the road and asked the driver to stop. We spoke with half a dozen armed men stationed there.

"Those look more like clarinets than guns," Charlotte said. The guns had long barrels that flared into bell-shaped bottoms. When the bells tilted up, we saw rings of holes for bullets at the base.

"I think they're using guns that we left behind in Afghanistan," said Charlotte, referring to a time when the British fought there. "They must be a hundred years old."

The men explained that an attack was under way in Qurgonteppa. They said the Russians had given tanks to the men's enemies. The men prepared a defence in case the tanks broke through Qurgonteppa and tried to sweep up the highway to Dushanbe.

Charlotte had been commissioned to write a shopping feature, not a war story, and I was on holiday, with no clear objective in mind and no deadline to meet. Driven forward by journalistic habit, a need to see firsthand what would occur, Charlotte and I decided to try to reach Qurgonteppa.

I did not feel afraid. Charlotte and I left our driver behind and hitchhiked instead. We stood at the side of the road with our thumbs out. Soon a cotton truck stopped. The driver offered us a lift. A young couple already sat in the trailer. We joined them, all cross-legged, clutching the sides, as we rattled down the highway. We chatted briefly, but before long a car flashed its lights at us and the truck driver did a U-turn. He dropped us back at the opposition post. We stood by the road again with our thumbs out. This time a Lada carrying police officers stopped. They said they would travel through Qurgonteppa on their way to the Afghan border. We climbed into the car.

We continued down the road. Every vehicle that we passed flashed its lights at us. Then we heard the sound of what might have been a shell exploding. *"Nazad,"* I yelped and hoped, as instructed, that the driver would turn back. He took us to the opposition post. That sound scared me. I felt a rush of adrenaline and realized a fast return to Dushanbe now was the obvious choice. Our original driver had waited and remained loyal to strangers who took a big risk.

We joined the column of refugees that fled for safety. We glanced back at the guard post and saw some fighters running out, shouting, "What are we going to do?" What chance did clarinet guns have against tanks? We left with our driver, consumed with guilt, and felt certain the opposition fighters would be slaughtered when the tanks broke through.

In Dushanbe we picked up our shopping and kept an appointment at the American embassy. We had booked it for a background briefing. The political officer interrupted us once we told him what we had seen. He ran to file a report.

At the airport we found that all flights had been cancelled. We dragged our bags and looked for a taxi. One driver agreed on a fare to take us to the border. On the way, we stopped at a shop. Charlotte went in to try to buy water but came out with a plastic bag full of matches. I could not stop laughing.

"But we can't get them in Kiev," she said. I told her that she had turned into a Soviet person, carrying fifty match boxes across Central Asia.

When we reached the border, we paid our taxi driver and then joined hundreds of refugees who were crossing into Uzbekistan on foot. Weighed down with sacks of shopping, we faced a long walk. I felt guilty. Charlotte now struggled under the weight of packages that she had wanted to leave behind. We had no hands free to help refugees carry possessions from homes they had to leave.

All flights at the local airport on the Uzbek side of the border had also been cancelled. Several taxi drivers queued by the border post. We booked a car for Samarkand, the nearest Uzbek city with a sizeable airport that might have flights to Kiev. I thought of home, but we still faced a sixteen-hour trip by car and uncertainty at the airport.

As the hours passed, the landscape became dry and empty. We had entered the Qizilqum desert. We saw few other cars. We passed time by telling each other stories about our childhood summers. I longed for our family cottage, for a clear, clean lake that churned up whitecaps like a mini-sea on windy days. There was no sign of water here. Charlotte spoke of summers she had spent with her cousins at their castle in Scotland on windswept moors. Her story was interrupted by a guard who stopped us at a checkpoint.

He carried a gun and ordered us out of the taxi with all our bags. We struggled into the guard's cabin. It was sparsely furnished with two narrow beds and one small side table. Sand swirled in through the doorway as we moved. No traffic passed by now. I doubted that any would for several hours.

"Sit," the guard ordered. I obeyed and sat on one bed. Charlotte sat on the other. I felt very afraid. I did not like the sight of beds. We had left no paper trail behind for the borders that we crossed. No one knew where we were. We could easily disappear in this desert. The only witness would be the taxi driver, who was a stranger. I did not even know if he was still waiting for us. The guard might have ordered him to leave. Two of us faced one guard, but he had a gun and we did not.

For once, Charlotte and I did not talk. We remained quiet and compliant. I thought through questions the guard might ask and how best to answer them. I felt comforted by the thought of that agent who had followed us through Tashkent hotels and tailed us all the way to our colleague's house. The security services must by now know who we were and where we went and know that we posed no threat.

The door slammed; the guard entered the room again.

"Documents," he ordered. We gave him our passports.

"Visas." We gave him papers for Kiev. I included my accreditation card. I hoped official status there would help in some way here. I could not judge the character of this guard. His monosyllabic orders left no opening for conversation, no way to strike up a rapport with him.

Hours passed. Still Charlotte and I barely talked. I felt calmer now. The guard left and did not lock the door, though where could we really run in this desert where there was still no traffic on the road?

Toward dusk the guard returned. He questioned us briefly. Where had we been? Why were we here? I told him the truth and hoped he would believe me. I emphasized shopping. I downplayed our trip south to Qurgonteppa. The guard left. He returned about an hour later.

"Go," he said. He had not asked for a bribe.

We saw the taxi parked by the post. The driver sat inside. Had he stayed out of loyalty to us or had he been ordered to do so? We did not know and did not ask. We were just grateful for a ride to Samarkand.

The receptionist at the Intourist hotel in Samarkand did not ask us any questions. We received a big room with a view and no hassle. We spread our shopping across one bed and admired it. Charlotte wrapped a recently purchased scarf around her head, put on her coat and gloves, opened the window and held my shortwave radio out so that we could listen to a BBC news broadcast. Cold air swirled into the room. The newsreader spoke of pitched battles, lives lost in Tajikistan. I thought of our driver from the market and his relatives in Qurgonteppa, as well as the fighters with clarinet guns; some must be dead, and the country was in such a mess.

Charlotte switched the radio off. We shut the window. The room warmed up quickly. We thought of home. I would soon leave for London. Friends in Kiev had arranged a goodbye party for me and had stockpiled wine and food for the occasion. Would we make it back on time?

Exhausted from our travels, we slept. In the morning we went to the airport to inquire about flights. Tickets remained cheap – about four dollars to fly across eleven time zones. We purchased two for every Kiev-bound flight over the next three days. The Aeroflot agent warned us of the likelihood that none would actually fly.

The first flight was scheduled for 3 a.m. the next day. At midnight we checked out of our hotel. By 4 a.m. we sat in a taxi heading back to the hotel as the flight had been cancelled.

Large, fluffy flakes of snow fell from the sky, and blanketed the road ahead. The taxi driver lost control of the car on the slippery road and smashed into a car in front of us. Unhurt but dazed, we took our luggage from the trunk and walked the rest of the way to the hotel. We paused to rest several times. Snow soon covered our coats and bags.

When we got to the hotel, the receptionist said that the room was still ours and gave us the key. We opened the door, flicked on the light and saw lumps in the beds. We recognized two women from the hotel staff. They sat up, surprised to see us. They were annoyed that they had to vacate the room, but they eventually left.

"They've stolen my tampons," Charlotte said. She had accidentally left a pack behind and had looked forward to reclaiming them.

The next morning we returned to the airport with our luggage. We hoped the morning flight might fly. The Aeroflot agent allowed us to hand in our tickets.

"So the flight's actually leaving," I asked.

"Of course," the agent said, no mention of fuel or cancelled flights. We sat in the departure lounge, feeling skeptical that the flight would leave. Then we heard a boarding call. We passed through security. A guard pulled us aside. He would not let us leave with so much shopping. He wanted a bribe. I fought and negotiated. I pointed out that everyone else was allowed through with a flotilla of suitcases and live poultry. Eventually I gave in and paid. I did not want to loose this rare chance to leave. The guard let us through to board the plane. Our flight went smoothly and we landed in Kiev on time.

Bill hosted my goodbye party at his apartment. I looked around the room filled with friends I had made over the past two years, the bonds so strong; I would not have survived without these people and would miss so many of them. Newcomers came as well. We met for the first and last time. Wine flowed, music played, smokers clustered on the balcony, a chill in the October air.

At noon the next day, my Lada so fully loaded that I could barely see, I waved goodbye to Charlotte, who remained behind, and Stephen, who would move into my flat. I drove down Khreshchatyk, remembering my first drive along it with Mary when police officers had stopped us on every block. They had asked why our husbands let us out in the car alone, wanted to know how I had learned to drive and also asked for bribes. No one stopped me now. I took the highway west. Lviv and Hungary lay ahead.

Now that I was no longer focused on work, I could appreciate the landscape for its beauty. The Carpathian Mountains were ablaze in autumn colours. At the Ukrainian-Hungarian border, guards searched the car. One saw a coin that he said I could not take out of the country. Unaware of this, I handed him the coin, but he refused to take it and said, "If anyone asks, just say you threw it in a field."

I did not know that I felt stressed until I picked my way across the final kilometre of potholed Ukrainian roads and crossed safely into Hungary. I loved Ukraine and my friends there, but it was still enough of an arbitrary and unpredictable place that nothing, not even the right to leave, could be taken for granted. When I heard my first *Jó napot kívánok* [good day], a Hungarian greeting on Hungarian soil, I felt set loose, free.

A few kilometres inside Hungary I saw a brightly lit service station. It seemed like such a novelty to drive up to a pump in the middle of nowhere and fill up. I opened my trunk, took out four metal gasoline tins and a funnel. I thought that I should fill the tins, even though I realized that I no longer needed to.

I left the tins, which had been such important survival tools these past two years, by the pump, and looked back, feeling anxious without them.

I walked back and forth through the entrance to the service station store a dozen times, mesmerized by the automatic doors that opened and closed with a swoosh each time. I stood in front of the store wall decked with windshield wipers, pressure gauges and all sorts of automobile paraphernalia in packages that hung from hooks. I stared and wondered what to buy, then realized that I needed nothing. Roadside service existed here. But hoarding is a hard habit to break. I ended up taking windshield wipers and a timing belt to the cash. Before the attendant rung them in, I stopped her and placed the items back on their hooks.

The payphone outside worked. There were no crackles on the Budapest line when I called Anna. I sped through the Hungarian countryside partly because I could. No potholes jolted the car. No flying gravel cracked the windscreen. The roads ran straight. None ended in a ditch or unmarked construction site. Mostly, though, I sped because I wanted to see Anna, Gyula and their children as soon as possible.

We spent a leisurely three days together, walking through central Budapest, visiting old haunts and catching up on developments in one another's lives. I looked up more friends. Everyone seemed well. When it was time to leave one friend travelled with me as far as Germany. We parted company there and I continued the rest of the way on my own, driving my Lada onto the ferry for the channel crossing to England. Once we arrived I had to adjust to driving on the left side of the road with a car designed for driving on the right. As I approached London, I thought of my new life there. Charlotte was doing well professionally. She reported for the *Observer* on the war in

Bosnia, spending long periods in Sarajevo, a city under siege. I admired her courage.

I would sublet Charlotte's room. We would share it on her brief trips back. I lived in the centre of the city, somewhere on the border between Bayswater and Westbourne Grove. Shops lined the streets everywhere that I walked. I felt so overwhelmed my first day out. I tried to buy groceries for dinner. In one store I stood by a shelf – goods stretched down a long row; there was too much choice. I had to leave. In the next store I tried the produce section – lettuce, tomatoes, snow peas, asparagus, star fruit, mangoes, beans, peppers and so much more. I could not make up my mind about what to buy. In the end, I chose one cucumber and left. I paid in cash. I ate fast food falafel on the way home.

IO

CHECHNYA IN LONDON

I began work the next day at my new job in radio journalism at the BBC. This would be my first desk job in an office. I wondered how I would adjust. I felt nervous on the bus ride in.

I checked in at the front desk and received a pass. I crossed a courtyard, walked through a warren of corridors and took an elevator up to my floor. I noticed Ron as soon as I entered my new office. I had been hired to replace him. Ron would leave in a few days on a foreign correspondent posting.

Ron did not see me. He was on the phone and sat with his back to the door on a chair behind his desk in a glass cubicle. The cubicle's glass walls stopped a few feet short of the ceiling, so all that Ron said flowed out overtop. His cubicle was situated on one side of an otherwise large, open room filled with desks, headsets and reel-to-reel tape decks mounted on wheels. Stubs of blue chalk and razor blades (tools for editing tape) lay scattered across the tape machines and desks. Newspapers were piled up in corners.

When Ron hung up the phone, he swivelled around.

"Welcome," he said, surprised. "Is it nine o'clock already?" He leaped out of his chair, came out of his glass cubicle and shut the door behind him. It closed with a loud click.

"No!" he said and turned back around. He tried the door. It was locked. We could see his keys on the desk through the glass.

"Excuse me," Ron said. Then he pulled a table toward the cubicle, climbed on it and over the top of the glass wall and landed with a thud on the other side. He unlocked the door and came back out. I would have to be careful with the door. At five foot four, I stood no chance of scaling that wall.

We sat and chatted. Ron briefed me about my new job. I told him about developments in Ukraine, Moldova and Central Asia. Others drifted into the office. One by one Ron introduced me – Gennady, Gregori, Lara, and then a name that I remembered for not being Russian, Alison. She was one of the only non-Russians in the office. I identified with her. If I understood what Ron said well, I had been hired as a link between this world of Russia in London and the main English-language newsroom. I would filter news, cull Russian information gathered here and package it into stories for a non-Russian audience and analyze events. I would be a bridge.

Ron and the others went back to work. I waited for my formal orientation, scheduled later in the morning. I sat at an empty desk with the daily papers. As I stared at the headlines, my mind wandered. I thought about this life that I began in a city that I knew so well. I had spent time here as a child with relatives and family friends. I had studied here, returned regularly from Hungary and Ukraine, but this time felt different. I had a job and since I also held a British passport, I could settle in London and make the transition from expat to immigrant.

Alison returned with a large set of headphones around her neck. She plugged them into a tape deck, swivelled tape, cut sections with a razor blade and taped the ends together. I heard her chat in what seemed to be flawless Russian with colleagues.

When she had finished editing her tape, I complimented Alison on her Russian and asked how she learned to speak it so well.

"I studied it at university and spent time in Moscow. I met my husband over there, so I have an advantage. I can speak Russian at home," Alison said. She told me a little bit about her husband, Gagik.

"He's Armenian," she said.

"Armenia! That's one republic I never visited," I told her. "I'd love to go. I hear they have the most extraordinary old churches. I've been to a lot of places nearby in the Caucasus. I was in Chechnya almost exactly a year ago and Azerbaizhan last month."

Alison cut me off with a laugh, "Don't tell an Armenian you've been to Azerbaizhan. They hate each other!" Then Alison rushed off to the studio with her tape. She had a deadline to meet.

Not long afterwards I sat in my glass cubicle and read notes about an unusual development in Chechnya. Even though it had won that showdown with Russia when I visited – Russian troops pulled back – Chechnya was still part of Russia. No state recognized Chechen independence. Now I read that Chechnya had appointed a prime minister and sent him to England. This Chechen prime minister, Ruslan Outsiev, arrived in London with his brother, Nazarbek, to arrange for Chechen passports and a Chechen currency and postage stamps to be printed. He was also establishing an embassy in London for Chechnya.

"Won't Russia go ballistic?" I asked a colleague. He nodded and rushed into a studio. Later I heard that Alison had interviewed Ruslan.

"You can't throw that out," my sister, Deborah, said as politely as she could but clearly shocked that I had put an empty tin in the garbage can instead of the recycling bin.

Ashamed, I asked her to explain recycling rules. None had existed when I last lived at home. I had to learn on this trip back for Christmas. It was a small matter but a reminder that places change and can't be taken for granted.

Deborah and I finished tidying the kitchen. Our father came in.

"Anyone for a ski?" he asked. He already wore his toque and coat. Our golden retriever, Chester, stood by the door, tail wagging, ears cocked, happy and impatient to get going.

"Coming," I said. We got our skis out of the garage. Chester lay on the ground outside. He gnawed on a chunk of ice. My father and I put skis over our shoulders, held both poles in one hand and walked down a small path to the lake at the bottom of my parents' housing complex. A trail ran around the lake. We stopped at the trail, slid our boots into bindings, strapped our poles around our wrists and skied down a small embankment onto the snow-covered frozen lake, the sky overhead blue and cloudless.

Chester, already far in the distance, came racing back. He tried to catch the tips of my skis as I slid forward. He enjoyed his game. The crisp, cold air made me shudder until I built up a sweat, but it suited him well in his heavy coat of golden winter fur. I missed moments like this. I felt at home on this small lake with my father and his dog. I wondered if it was time to come back but could not find answers to the usual questions that rattled round in my head. Where would I live? What would I do? Would I be bored? I worried for a moment about being caught between the world of London and this world of home, and that I might not fit in properly in either. I pushed these thoughts away. I caught up with my father. We rested for a few minutes on the other side of the lake. Chester lay beside us. He was using his teeth to dislodge ice caught between the pads of his paws. My father pulled a small tape recorder from his jacket pocket.

"What do you think this is?" he asked as he pressed Play. I heard a familiar sound that I could not place.

"Footsteps on snow," he said, so pleased that he had captured it on tape. I wished I could take that sound back with me to London.

"Just over for a holiday?" the taxi driver asked as we pulled away from Heathrow, onto the motorway that led to central London. "When are you heading back?"

"I live here," I said, still surprised to be asked this question, though it happened all the time.

"Pigeonholed by your accent," Deborah had commented when I had told her I could never escape it. We had fit in so well as children, visiting relatives with our mother who was born in Wales and studied medicine in London. Alone, I was viewed as yet one more foreigner on holiday here.

I dragged my bags up flights of long narrow stairs to the top floor of a row house that I shared with Stewart, Charlotte's flat mate. Charlotte was still in Bosnia. I flicked the light on, dropped my bags in the bedroom and then wove through a pathway between stacks of old newspapers in the living room, walked down a few steps and along a corridor into the kitchen. Half a dozen bottles of wine – each one almost half finished, as per Stewart's daily habit – lined the kitchen counter. I opened the fridge. It was empty. Stewart must still be away.

I made a cup of tea and sat in silence. I stared at the phone and wanted to call someone, to hear a friendly voice welcome me back, but I did not really have friends here, just colleagues. All of my friends lived somewhere else. I went to buy groceries and for a swim. The day slipped away.

The next morning I arrived early at work. I went down to the canteen for coffee. Back in our office, I sat at a large desk with my coffee and spread the morning papers across it. I loved this part of the day, the breadth of coverage in the papers here, especially for foreign news. I heard footsteps in the hallway and looked up as my first colleague arrived. I saw his thumb, wrapped in a huge padded white bandage, enter first, then the rest of this man.

"What happened!" I asked. He explained that another colleague had slammed this colleague's thumb in the door. The reason for the feud and ensuing injury was so complex that I could not follow it, but I did understand that hatred lingered and this thumb – almost a trophy now – marked him as the victim in what he considered an unjust office war.

As lonely as I sometimes felt, I think my Russian colleagues had it worse. At least I now heard my native language everywhere and had relatives in the U.K. My Russian colleagues had left so many family members and friends behind when they moved to London. They only functioned in their own language at work, though I guessed now that Russian world could be small and fraught. Oh well, I would never understand it. I turned back to my paper. Soon our office hummed again. Everyone was back at work.

* * *

One morning I sat in my glass cubicle. I heard a conversation between two colleagues that floated in over top.

"He's been arrested – both men are dead. They think that he might have worked for the KGB, though they don't know who actually pulled the trigger," one said.

"Where's Alison?" asked the other.

"She's not here. She must be at home, in shock." I heard many personal conversations at work, but even when I heard each word in hushed exchanges and could not help but piece together private affairs I pretended to know nothing unless directly told. Too curious now, I rushed out of my cubicle.

"What happened?" I asked the men who stood nearby. They said that Alison's husband, Gagik, had been arrested for involvement in the murder of the visiting Chechen prime minister, Ruslan Outsiev, and his brother Nazarbek.

I could not believe what I heard. I just stood there and listened. I did not know what to say. Our boss came into the room. He looked grave.

"Meeting in five minutes," he said. Then he left to find others.

In the room next door, a few people sat on desk tops but most of us stood as our boss summarized the facts. The police were holding Gagik and his friend Mkritch on suspicion of murdering Ruslan and Nazarbek. He told us not to talk to the press – an awkward instruction for a room full of journalists.

I lingered in the hallway after the meeting. People stood in clusters and exchanged information. Everyone worried about Alison. No one had been in touch with her. Someone told me that Gagik had worked as a translator for Ruslan and that Alison helped arrange an invitation for Mkritch so that he could travel from Armenia to London.

Deadlines loomed. A producer rushed by. Someone snatched a directory of employee home addresses and phone numbers from a tabletop and shoved it away in a desk drawer. Of course, we'd have to be careful now. Alison's home address and phone number were listed in that directory, always confidential information, now more confidential than before. We drifted back to work. I sat at my desk and completed a morning assignment my mind only half on it, my thoughts still with Alison.

On the way back from lunch, I showed my identity card as I passed the security desk at the front door, went up to my office, dropped my coat and left for a meeting. When I returned late that afternoon, Charlotte sat at my desk. She was back from Bosnia for a few days.

"Hello," she said.

"What are you doing here?" I replied. "How did you get in?" I did not really need to ask. Charlotte had enough charm and journalistic skill to disarm any guard.

"They've put me on the story. I'm the only one who's been to Chechnya," she said. So I was pitted now against my friend. I thought, though, that this served me right after all these years of prying into the lives of others for quotes and information.

"I'm sorry, but I can't tell you anything, not that I really know much anyway." We left the office together, crossed the road and waited at a stop for our bus home. Black cabs whizzed past, faint drizzle visible in their headlights from moisture-laden air not quite filled with rain but more like mist from a cloud. A red double-decker arrived. We climbed the steps up to the top and sat near the front. Below, commuters inched their way home on crowded London streets.

"Do you think she knew about Gagik?" Charlotte asked.

"I wondered about a boyfriend that I had over there, so I'm sure that Alison did as well. But once you know someone for a while the doubts fade. They never disappear, but they slip to the back of your mind," I said.

"Well, Gagik must have been a bloody good actor," Charlotte said.

"I know. What horrible deceit."

"Do you think Alison ever suspected?" Charlotte asked.

"I don't know, but I can't imagine that she did," I replied. "I think he probably used her. Or maybe he was blackmailed and didn't know what to do." I asked Charlotte if she remembered Mykola, a journalist in Kiev. She did.

"I remember advice that he gave me so well. He said, 'Never date a man from here – they're only after one thing, your passport. I know how they think.' I thought those words a bit harsh and cynical back then."

"But Alison's situation might be even worse than that," Charlotte said.

As the days passed my colleagues and I learned more about Alison, Gagik and Mkritch from news coverage. I also felt increasingly distanced from Alison. Stories written in a familiar journalistic formula turned Alison into someone barely recognizable – she seemed more a character in a murder mystery novel than a real person. I pieced her story together from what I read.

Alison and Gagik lived in Chiswick, a neighbourhood in West London not far from Heathrow Airport. Gagik worked as a swimming pool attendant. In the Soviet Union he had been involved in an art venture with Mkritch.

Alison helped Gagik launch business ventures in London. They shipped clothes and computers to the Soviet Union through companies they set up, Alga International and Orient Line. I remembered my own shopping deprivation and that urge to buy when goods appeared in shops. Alison and Gagik's businesses could succeed, but so many others had the same idea that competition would be intense.

I read that Ruslan was thirty-eight and Nazarbek, a boxer and very fit, was twenty. The papers provided more details. In the days immediately following Gagik and Mkritch's arrest, articles described the Chechens' lavish lifestyle. I sat at my desk with a cup of coffee from the canteen downstairs scarcely able to process what I read, so fantastic did it seem.

Ruslan and Nazarbek bought a centrally located penthouse in Marylebone, not far from Madame Tussaud's and the Sherlock Holmes Museum, for £750,000 in cash. They purchased furniture at Harrods. One bed bought there cost £9,000. Ruslan and Nazarbek's cash resources exceeded anything that I had imagined – their source of wealth must have been Chechen oil.

Their dining habits seemed equally extravagant. Some restaurant bills totalled £2,000. One waiter quoted in a news article said the brothers tipped him £100 for a meal. They also allegedly hired expensive prostitutes, several in one night.

My mind wandered a lot at work during those early post-arrest days. I joined huddles with my colleagues in the hallways. We shared information that we read and tried to understand what had happened. I wondered how Gagik reacted. Was he jealous? Did he want a life like that? What did he learn translating for Ruslan? What shocked us most, though, was information about Ruslan's secret agenda in London, a mission to purchase two thousand Stinger anti-aircraft missiles. Some Russians in our unit considered this misinformation deliberately planted in newspapers. Others believed it, but could not agree on a motive for the purchase. My knowledge lagged behind that of my Russian colleagues, who had learned about Stingers during the Soviet invasion of Afghanistan. I did not know much about these weapons, so I researched them to learn more.

I collected news articles and documents about Stingers and stacked them on the floor beside my bed. Charlotte had returned to Bosnia, so I had the room to myself again. For several evenings I lay on the floor with a highlighter pen in one hand and flipped through the material. This research interested me more than my day job, where I often clock-watched, unable to adjust to the humdrum pace of desk work, bolting from the office at 5 p.m. sharp.

I initially focused on U.S. sources as Stingers originated in the United States. They are about four feet long and designed for portability. In various accounts, fighters carried Stingers and propped them on their shoulders to shoot down planes and helicopters. Heat-seeking guidance systems and ultraviolet detection that locked on targeted aircraft meant that even a fighter with average aim could score good hits. Stingers now circulated on the black market and knock-offs were also being manufactured.

I thought at once of General Dudayev in Chechnya. Russia had tried to intervene in Chechnya when it sent troops in by plane. The Chechens encircled the plane and trapped the soldiers. General Dudayev, with his airforce background, would understand better than most the enormous strategic advantage for his own forces if they could be armed with Stingers to counter any Russian advances by air.

But the vast number of weapons did not make sense. I only understood the size of the deal Ruslan tried to negotiate after more research. One report said that the United States had manufactured about fifty thousand Stingers since 1981. This meant that Ruslan, from tiny Chechnya, tried to buy the equivalent of 4 percent of all U.S.-made Stingers in more than a decade.

Then I tried to calculate the value of the deal. The U.S. report said that Stinger missiles sold for $200,000 on the black market in Pakistan. A purchase of two thousand Stinger missiles could have cost as much as $400 million, though knock-offs or a bulk order might have reduced the price. No matter what the discount, this deal involved a huge amount of money.

At work no one quite forgot about Alison and Gagik but, with daily deadlines, our focus shifted, time passed. I flew home to Canada for summer holidays. I stayed with my parents at our cottage in Québec. Deborah and our brother, Mark, joined us. Cousins who owned cottages close to ours dropped by. Babies bounced on knees. This next generation still caught me by surprise. I could not believe that a cousin I had grown up with was now old enough to have kids.

When our cousins left, we bought plates and glasses in from the verandah. My mother and Deborah went back out with books. My father and Mark watched tennis on TV in the living room. I went down to the dock for a swim. Chester, uninvited, came along. I would have to swim quickly. If he caught up, he would try to retrieve me. When I finished swimming, I floated in an inflatable dingy that my father had bought. Chester jumped on board. We drifted quietly until he spotted a fish and leaped out. This time I did not tip but floated on, water lapping against the boat, sleepy in the warmth of the sun. It was hard not to be seduced by thoughts of coming home. I would return one day, just not now. When my holiday was over, I flew back to London.

* * *

In October 1993, exactly one year after I had moved to London from Kiev, Gagik was in the papers again, this time for his sentencing. My colleagues and I followed these developments through news articles and read more details in that grizzly murder mystery that I could scarcely believe was Alison's life, and wished was not.

Court documents said that after Gagik learned about the Stinger negotiations, he contacted Mkritch. Reporters described Mkritch as an agent for the Armenian KGB. This was confusing terminology since the KGB technically did not exist anymore. The reporters confirmed that Alison had helped Mkritch obtain a visa and find an apartment, but indicated that she did not know of his security service ties or anything about the murder plot that unfolded between Gagik and Mkritch. I felt relieved when I read this but also felt badly – she had really been used.

At work no one had time to digest all the news, so we swapped details over coffee in the canteen. I learned that Ruslan accused Gagik of stealing £20,000 and also read that Ruslan planned to pass some or all of the Stingers onto Azerbaizhan, then involved in a conflict with Armenia. Both Gagik and Mkritch were Armenian. I wondered if personal allegiances contributed to their motivation.

Once Mkritch arrived in London, events proceeded quickly. Mkritch said in a police statement that he met with Ruslan and asked him to abandon the missile deal. Ruslan refused. Mkritch then contacted his bosses in the security services. They ordered Ruslan's assassination. They anticipated this could spark a blood feud, common in Chechnya, so they also wanted Nazarbek killed as a precautionary measure. Otherwise he would try to avenge his brother's death.

I kept a binder filled with information on the case. One article quoted Mkritch telling police, "The murders were planned by the KGB. I had no choice but to obey the KGB. They would have harmed my family."

Mkritch and his bosses discussed various options and decided to contract a hit man in Los Angeles for the job. Chechen gangs would be blamed for the murder, a plausible cover story given Ruslan's history as a racketeer and Chechen gangs' notoriety for revenge attacks. This plan failed when the U.K. denied the hit man from Los Angeles a visa.

Mkritch and his bosses consulted further. Eventually Mkritch's bosses ordered that he shoot Ruslan and Nazarbek. They would provide false passports, visas and misinformation for a cover story that the Chechen brothers had returned to Russia.

"Now I understand the whole idea was to put me as a victim and finish the case," Mkritch told police.

Mkritch did not want to kill Ruslan and Nazarbek himself. He said that an assassin was hired. A young American smuggled the murder weapon, a gun, into Britain. A man named Arthur received the gun. Prosecutors in the murder case described what happened next.

In late February 1993, Nazarbek checked into a London hospital for treatment of a sinus condition. He was expected home four days later. With Nazarbek, Ruslan's brother and bodyguard out of the way, the assassin went to work. He arrived at the brothers' flat and shot Ruslan at point-blank range in bed while Ruslan slept. Mkritch said Gagik was present but did not take part in the murder.

When Nazarbek came back, he did not seem to notice anything unusual. He went to bed, fell asleep and the assassin struck again. He shot Nazarbek, like Ruslan, three times in the head with a Beretta pistol. Mkritch said the murder weapon was smuggled back to the United States. One key piece of evidence disappeared, but the bodies remained.

I wondered if Alison had sensed a change in her husband after this – erratic behaviour or anxiety. The prosecutor said Gagik and Mkritch moved quickly to eliminate traces of the murders. They bought a new bed to replace one soaked through with blood. They also purchased a refrigerator. Then they called delivery men Patrick Johnson and Patrick Marsh and offered them £500 if they would move a large box from the Chechens' penthouse to a semi-detached house in Harrow.

When the delivery men commented on the heavy weight of the box, Mkritch told them that it contained a seventeenth-century statue. Gagik said the box contained a refrigerator. Markings on the packaging seemed to confirm this, but Johnson and Marsh became suspicious.

"Four of us were trying to lift it. It was heavy and if it was a fridge-freezer it shouldn't have been that heavy," Johnson told the court. "It smelled like a fridge-freezer where everything's gone rotten inside. There was a sort of lavender fragrance to camouflage whatever the smell was." After the move, the delivery men telephoned the police. Police officers went to the house in Harrow, searched it, and found the box. When they opened it, they discovered Ruslan's body inside. He still wore his pyjamas and earplugs. His body had been bound with tape, rolled in a carpet and then stuffed into the box. These details must have horrified Alison as she listened in the courtroom; they certainly horrified me.

The police went to the Chechens' penthouse. They found Nazarbek's body. Then they staked out the building. The next day Mkritch and Gagik arrived with an electric saw and plastic bags. I shuddered as I imagined what might have ensued had the police not intervened. They arrested Mkritch and Gagik and collected evidence to convict the men.

I next read with concern that Alison had been briefly arrested. News reports stated that the police had intercepted a vial sent from Los Angeles with a destination address of Alison's house in West London. The vial contained enough snake poison to kill a hundred people. Reports differed on one key point. Some said that Alison had ordered the venom and was released because she could legally possess it. I did not believe this. Other reports stated that someone else had sent the venom to Alison, a more likely explanation, I thought.

Mkritch also had snake poison. He kept it under a bandage on his body. Police found it when they arrested Mkritch. They identified that type of venom as a poison of choice for security service agents from Mkritch's part of the world who might need to commit suicide. Mkritch succeeded even without his vial. He hanged himself in prison. Just before his death he told police: "The KGB would not forgive anyone at any time. By talking about these matters now, perhaps I am signing a death warrant for my family."

Gagik faced trial at the Old Bailey alone. Alison looked on from the gallery. The defence portrayed Gagik as an incompetent body disposer. It argued that he did not participate in the murders. The prosecution said that Gagik helped plan each stage. The detective inspector in charge of the case, Julian Headon, cited greed as a motive.

Headon said that Gagik "was doing business with Ruslan. He knew all the contacts; Ruslan could not speak English and with him out of the way the Chechen government would either have to start again or let Gagik carry on with the [Stinger] deals." According to Headon, "Ruslan's death would have put Gagik into the big money . . . Millions upon millions of pounds."

The court reached no verdict on who actually pulled the trigger. The judge described the killings as "professional assassinations" and told Gagik, "There is no real reason to believe that your hand was on the trigger. The murders appear to have been planned in this country by Martirossian [Mkritch]."

Gagik received two life sentences for double murder. I read, with sadness, that Alison cried as Gagik was led away to jail. I could not imagine the pain of discovering that your husband had led such a double life.

Stephen had arrived back from Ukraine. We were colleagues now in the same unit at work. I felt so happy to have his company here in my middle world, halfway between home and Kiev. He rented a flat in Chiswick, where Alison and Gagik had lived. I went for dinner one evening, strolled through this green and pleasant neighbourhood and thought of Alison again. I had heard that she'd moved in with her sister, Karen.

I reached Stephen's apartment and rang the bell. He came to the door holding a wooden spoon. I followed him into the kitchen. Pots bubbled on the stove top. I smelled simmering tomatoes, garlic and basil.

"I'm not kidding. He said, 'Gobble, gobble' to me," I told Stephen as I described a conversation that I'd had that morning with our manager. He stirred a pot while I watched and sipped wine.

"What does that mean?" Stephen said laughing.

"He said something about sacrificing a turkey for Christmas. I think they're getting ready for job cuts."

"That can't be. They've just hired," he said.

We switched topics. We discussed films and gossiped about friends in Kiev. I asked Stephen about his girlfriend Katya. They had met in Ukraine and planned to marry and build a life in England. I felt adrift compared to Stephen and Katya. The only real decision I had made was that even though I liked London, I did not want to settle here. I wasn't sure that I would ever be fully accepted. A few weeks later I flew home for Christmas.

When I arrived back at work after the holidays, I saw an ad for a Kiev correspondent in our internal newsletter. I applied for the position. The next weeks passed in a blur of work during the day and study at night. I had to pass a newsroom test in order to qualify for the job. At home, I spread a map of the world across the kitchen table, memorized countries and their capitals, feeling that I was back at school again. Then I gathered key facts about each country and learned those as well. I passed the exam and prepared for the board interview.

At the end of February 1994, I found out that I got the job. Excited at the prospect of fieldwork once more, I shed belongings I had gathered in London and tuned my Lada for a return journey across Europe, back over the Carpathians to Ukraine. As I prepared for my trip, I heard that Alison had had an encounter with the police. She issued a copyright violation writ against them for a picture published without her permission. Alison's mother had taken the picture. It showed Alison in a bikini. I did not know what to make of this but really now thought only of my move.

One morning in early April I stood outside our flat – a line of boxes stretched down the pavement, filled with tinned food and spices, books, clothes, posters and other items to make the place that I would rent in Kiev feel more like home. I tried to load the boxes in the car, pushed and squeezed, admitted defeat, removed a few, put them back in the flat and then finally slammed the back door shut for good, afraid to open it again in case the contents tumbled out.

Once I had cleared space around the driver's seat, I turned the ignition, slid into first gear and felt the most enormous sense of freedom. I was on my way again.

I drove south toward the Dover ferry port. On board, I watched England recede, then disappear, as the ferry churned its way across the channel. I soon forgot London and looked forward to returning to Kiev with excitement, sped through France, Germany and Austria, and felt a surge of emotion at the Hungarian border, surprised by my attachment to a country where I had no family and no real roots. I reached Moskva tér in the centre of Budapest and parked my car outside Anna and Gyula's building. I walked into the courtyard, which was unchanged. I had crossed it so many times before seven years ago, always holding the morning papers. I crossed it again now and reached Anna and Gyula's apartment. I rang the bell. Gyula opened the door. "Zsuzsi! Szia!" he said with a warm grin and gave me a big hug. This was my home away from home. I had opted for the longer drive across Europe just for a moment like this.

Anna stood in the kitchen, unchanged, with that smile I remembered so well. She put my bags in the small room behind the kitchen, where I would sleep. Then we settled into the living room chairs, where we had sat so often before. Anna and Gyula discussed political developments in Hungary. Fidesz, the party that I so admired when I lived here, was now ruled by a man with a nationalist agenda. I felt alienated by this development. The economy had been generous to both Anna and

Gyula, who were well employed. Their life looked good. I felt happy just to sit with them as dusk fell on Budapest.

The next day we briefly toured the city. Shop windows brimmed with goods once considered luxury items. This more prosperous Budapest still had its old charm intact. In the afternoon we returned to Anna and Gyula's apartment. I packed my small bag and said goodbye. They stood on the sidewalk as I once more slid into the driver's seat of my Lada, cleared a wide enough tunnel through boxes for a rear-mirror view, waved and then sped out along the highway northeast toward Záhony. I became increasingly apprehensive as the hours passed and I approached the border crossing into Ukraine. I reached it at 9 p.m., the last in a small line of about six cars.

"The Foreign Ministry sent advance notice," the border guard said as he inspected my passport. I nearly melted with relief. He waved me through with barely a glance at the boxes stuffed in the back. My confidence soared. I spent so little time at the border that my ambition grew. Instead of stopping for the night close by at Uzhorod, I pressed on over the Carpathian Mountains toward Lviv, certain I could reach the city in less than three hours.

By 2 a.m. I realized my mistake. The car crawled up pitch-dark mountain roads pitted with trench-like potholes. I had forgotten the reality of road travel over here. By 3 a.m. I gave up and pulled over, the car so full I could not stretch out. I slumped over the steering wheel, threw a quilt over my head and woke four hours later when the sun peeped in through a crack in the cover. Two men stood in front of the car. There was no one else in sight on this deserted stretch of road. The men smoked and looked relaxed. If they wanted to kill me, I thought they already would have smashed a window and done the deed, so I opened the door, got out and said hello.

"Not Polish," one said disappointedly when he heard my accent. They thought I was a trader who might sell them goods from my laden car. As we said goodbye that man muttered, "You have a problem," and pointed at a green trickle of fluid that leaked out from beneath my car. Every man here was an amateur mechanic, so I popped the hood and let him jiggle a pipe. The other man returned from a nearby stream with a jar of water that he poured into the radiator. "Don't stop again until you reach Kiev," he said. Skeptical, but grateful, I did as instructed and arrived there with no further mishap.

In the city centre, traffic jammed Khreshchatyk – a big change from 1990 when the roads had been nearly deserted. I reached my old street, turned onto it and drove up a hill, around a bend and along a route so filled with memories that nostalgia welled up in me. I belonged here. My new apartment stood across the street from the Foreign Ministry press office, where I first applied for accreditation, close by to many friends.

I met several for dinner that evening. We chatted about politics. Recent parliamentary elections, the first since independence, had proceeded well; a presidential election would follow in two months. The state seemed stable despite tensions that still simmered between Ukraine and Russia over the Black Sea fleet. I was back at work already. I relished my escape from a nine-to-five desk job, though I did not have quite the same freedom as I had when I last lived in Kiev.

I still had to go to an office for work. We had a studio in the centre. In this twenty-four-hour news operation the work day never ended. Some stories broke in the middle of the night. I would get up, check facts and report. The news machine must be fed.

I shared an office with Mykola, the journalist who gave me dating advice. I benefited from his knowledge and insight about politics in Ukraine, and enjoyed our friendship. Soon we hired younger reporters to help. They attended the news conferences. I began to spend more time in the studio than I wanted to and less time at events than before. I was in the office one June day, at my computer, when my boss, Zoya, called from London.

"I'll be in Kiev next week for a few days. Let's meet for dinner," she suggested.

I looked forward to her visit.

On the evening of Zoya's arrival we went out to a restaurant. Once we had ordered food, we exchanged news. I spoke of gossip related to the presidential election, a successful transition to a new leader and yet more proof of a stable state. She listened, interested, then asked. "Do you know about Alison?"

"No. What happened? Last I heard she'd moved in with her sister."

Zoya said that Alison and Karen lived in a town in Surrey, near London. Most of their neighbours worked for banks or security companies. She explained that Alison had returned to work and that her office routine remained unchanged. Colleagues respected her need for privacy. Sometimes she worked day shifts; other times, like everyone else, she worked nights.

Then Zoya said that one day police officers who were on patrol in Alison's town followed a driver in a red car who was behaving suspiciously. He circled around roads on the housing estate where Alison and Karen lived. The officers decided to stop the car. Zoya did not know the details, but we guessed the police flashed their lights or sounded a siren. Panic-stricken, perhaps, the driver rammed his car into a curb. Then he got out of the car and ran. He escaped from the police on foot.

The driver left items behind in the car, the two most significant being a gun and a map. The bullets in the gun had been hollowed out and filled with a mercury explosive, tipped with wax – a professional hit man, the police concluded.

The man had marked several places on his map. The police deduced that he intended to kill a housing estate resident. One theory held that the motive was robbery and the target, one of the bank or security company employees. The police also included Alison on their suspected victims list because of Gagik's murder convictions.

Five homes, including Alison and Karen's, were put under surveillance by the police. Technicians installed panic buttons. Police officers began armed patrols. They instructed residents not to open their doors if strangers knocked. I tried to imagine how Alison and her sister felt – terror at the possibility a hit man might be after them? Relief that he had come to the attention of the police and that they now had protection? Denial – perhaps the hit man wanted someone else? Zoya said that despite the scare, their daily routine remained as it had before.

At the end of April, on a Saturday, nearly a month after my arrival back in Kiev, Alison worked the night shift. Karen stayed at home. The doorbell rang. The person on the other side of the door identified himself as a pizza delivery man. Karen had not ordered pizza. She opened the door to tell him this. The man on the doorstep held a pistol. He shot Karen dead. Alison subsequently disappeared, presumably having been advised by the police to go into hiding.

I stopped eating. I had no appetite anymore. Zoya told me what little more she knew. The police believed the killer mistook Karen for Alison – they looked alike, with similar hair and glasses – and killed the wrong woman. After Zoya left, I asked a friend to fax me news coverage of the shooting and read a statement Alison had issued through the police: "I am deeply shocked and distraught by the death of my sister, Karen, who was murdered so horrifically simply because of her relationship to me." I thought of their parents, who had lost one daughter forever and the other to police protection. I felt so tired of violence.

It was part of life here as well. Something dark hung over Ukraine. I covered stories on baby smuggling in Western Ukraine, the arrival of the international drugs trade, the drop in life expectancy and the rise of HIV. I also felt the effects of a conflict between Russia and Ukraine over energy supplies. Ukraine could no longer afford to pay for imported Russian gas.

One night in early November, I sat in my kitchen. Our building had no heat yet. I turned the oven on full blast and closed the door to trap heat inside. I held a phone bill in my hand and looked at so many zeros tacked on to the end that I wondered how long it would take me to pay. I converted $US1 into *karbovanets* (the Ukrainian currency) and calculated the modest number of dollars I would need to pay the bill, set the money aside and went to bed.

I got up early the next morning. As I stepped out of my building, I saw an elderly woman ahead of me. She stood erect and wore a warm coat. A small dog tugged at the end of the leash that she held. The woman approached a dumpster. Then she stopped and looked in. I averted my eyes to protect her dignity. I had seen so many pensioners foraging in garbage cans. Their pensions could not keep pace with hyperinflation. When she had finished, I gave the woman some money. Both of us embarrassed, I hurried on.

I stood in line at a money exchange kiosque next door to where I used to live. I held a pillowcase in my hand. When I reached the kiosque window, I handed over dollars. The woman inside slowy counted *karbovanets*. I shovelled each huge pile she made into my pillowcase. When the transaction was finally over, I knotted the pillowcase closed and walked across the square to the post office. I joined a long line. When my turn came, the woman behind the counter counted each note. Finally she stamped my bill paid. Next month I would have to hire someone for this process. It took too much time.

I liked Kiev and my friends. For all the bad, I enjoyed life here, but somehow I wondered if by staying I was wasting time. The stories that I covered did not mean that much to me – a sewage plant that collapsed out east, a U.S. presidential visit, religious disputes. Time was on my mind when I returned home in the summer for another visit. I introduced my father, usually so forward-looking and engaged by new ideas, to the Internet.

"This is for the birds," he said when pages about golf, his favourite sport, loaded slowly over our cottage dial-up connection. I realized that my parents, although not quite old, were no longer young.

"I think I should go back, but I have no idea what I'd do," I told my friend James.

We sat in my kitchen in Kiev waiting for his two visitors. These American journalists would join us for dinner. James, a photographer, worked with them.

"Couldn't you report for Canadian TV or radio?" he asked.

"Maybe, but I'm not sure I want to stay in journalism. Before independence I felt that sometimes I discovered significant information no one else reported. Now stories are so routine," I told him. The doorbell rang. James's friends arrived. We poured wine for them. The visitors joined our conversation.

"Have you thought about international aid?" one of them asked. She told me about aid workers that she had met in Bosnia, how they brought food into Sarajevo during the siege and how they monitored prisoners' treatment to ensure it abided by the Geneva Conventions.

I had tried to volunteer for aid work after high school. I spent a year in Europe before university. An aid organization in Paris turned me away because at seventeen, I was still considered a child under French law.

I thought about our conversation in the weeks that followed and researched international aid organizations. I had no specific plan in mind but built a roster of contact numbers. As an experiment, I called one office and then another. Soon I had a series of interviews booked in London. I telephoned Stephen and told him that I would visit. He invited me to stay. In November I flew to London for the interviews and felt encouraged by the responses.

I heard the telephone ring early in the morning on my departure day. At first I thought it was my alarm clock. I had to leave early for my Kiev flight. Then I heard Stephen answer the phone. A minute later he knocked on my door.

"It's for you," he said. "It's your sister." I took the receiver. Deborah told me that our father had died from a brain aneurism. I hung up and sat on the sofa, unable to speak.

"Is there anything I can do to help?" Stephen asked. He booked me a flight home.

Deborah and Mark met me at the airport in Ottawa. We drove home to the emptiness of a fatherless house. Winter had set in and the light had disappeared. This was a bleak time of year under any circumstances in Canada. I still could not believe that my father, a fit, vibrant man, had died and that my mother would be alone. I missed my father so much. I felt a shift in generations and that my place was now back here.

I spoke to friends who had already lost a parent. I thought of Alison as well. She had disappeared after Karen died. I wondered if she had to cope with grief by herself, separated from family and friends.

My brother and sister went back to Toronto. I stayed with my mother. We went for walks, read the paper and looked after my father's new dog. I also phoned aid agencies in Canada to look for a job. International experience, which had been viewed as such an asset in London, was a liability here. I had no Canadian work experience. That was a big hurdle to surmount.

Back in Ukraine, those final months dragged. When my Kiev posting ended in June, I arranged for a three-month leave of absence. I spent it at the cottage with my mother. I wondered how I could return for good. In September, at the end of my leave of absence, I had no answer, so I flew back to London to work in the radio newsroom.

"Do you know any eligibles?" I asked Stephen one day. Not long afterwards he invited me for dinner with a guest from Australia named Sydney, my future husband. He was divorced, a year younger than me and an IT specialist.

Wine flowed as did talk of the Internet. I listened to his plans for websites, home servers, self-programmed databases, caught up in this wave of enthusiasm, amazed that a subject so different from politics excited me this much.

The next day Sydney called and invited me to the Tower of London. We toured the torture chamber. I wondered about this unusual spot for a first date. More followed in restaurants and cafés. We visited Morocco after Christmas.

"Two colonials who met in the Motherland," I told Sydney. I wondered if that's why we had clicked.

One huge problem loomed. I had already signed on with the International Federation of Red Cross and Red Crescent Societies (IFRC), through the British Red Cross. A staff member there said employment in Canada might be an option after work overseas. Offers for postings arrived. I stalled for as long as possible. I had to decide whether to quit my job and go or coast along in London.

"Have you ever thought about working overseas?" I asked Sydney one evening.

"I am overseas."

"I mean really overseas, somewhere completely different. You did call yourself a tumbleweed."

I had already turned down postings for singles in conflict zones, but this latest one in Sarajevo included sponsorship for a partner.

"Would you be willing to come?" I asked. "I won't go otherwise."

"Let me think about it," Sydney said. A few days passed and we did not discuss Sarajevo again. Then Sydney phoned after work. "I've done it," he said.

"Done what?"

"Told my boss I'm going. He said he'd have me back if I change my mind."

"Seriously? We're going to Sarajevo?" I said. When the conversation ended, I lay on my bed and imagined the future. I had never moved countries with someone else before. I felt happy, with one small doubt only. Sydney had lived a quiet life in Australia and England. What if he hated Sarajevo?

The next month passed quickly. We resigned from our jobs, packed our belongings, had medicals and booked our tickets.

I would leave first. Sydney was to follow a few weeks later. On an early June day we travelled out to Heathrow and toasted our new life over a drink in the bar. We had already planned a move back to Canada in a year. Boarding time came. We said goodbye. I slung my bag over my shoulder and walked to the departure lounge for my Sarajevo-bound flight, happy at the thought that I would soon meet Sydney at the other end.

II

BOSNIA

Bosnia-Herzegovina, a dramatic, mountainous country endowed with deep gorges and green valleys, showed scars of war on the descent toward Sarajevo. Roofless buildings, timbers black and broken, dotted the landscape. As the airplane swept low, I peered straight into the charred innards of what was once someone's home.

Military hardware dominated the runways. Helicopters landed, took off, circled or hovered in the air. I thought of *Apocalypse Now*.

Passengers trudged to the terminal and joined the line for passport control and customs. The line inched forward, but I cleared quickly, with none of the staring contests so typical of encounters with border officials in Ukraine. Two tall men stood out in the crowded arrivals hall. They held signs with the IFRC logo, offered a warm welcome and instant membership in their team.

We left the building and walked over to a car park. I saw yellow hazard tape everywhere. One of my colleagues loaded my luggage in the back. I pulled myself up into the passenger seat of a Land Cruiser designed for much bigger people. As we drove away from the airport, I noticed more areas marked off with hazard tape; my colleagues warned me that one of the most disturbing aspects of day-to-day life in Sarajevo was the mines left scattered through the city.

It was June 1997, eighteen months after Croat, Serb and Bosniac (Bosnian Muslim) leaders had signed the Dayton Peace Accord, which ended nearly four years of war. I was reminded once again of rules already drilled in to me at the head office in Geneva – mines still posed a major hazard; paved surfaces were the only safe place to walk.

I had a map of Sarajevo in my luggage. It showed the city surrounded by a ring of small, bright red dots. Each dot represented a minefield. Some of the dots crept down toward the centre; others stood scattered through unlucky neighbourhoods. Exploding yellow stars marked the site of "mine incidents," most likely where someone had lost a limb, or a life.

As we drove past Dobrinje, one of the worst affected areas, not far from the airport, I found it hard to imagine that life had once existed in this gutted, utterly ravaged, mine-ridden place. We turned onto the main road – sniper alley – that led into the centre of Sarajevo. It took no imagination at all to understand the impact of war on the outskirts. My colleagues told me that the teetering Oslobodjenie tower, which, we passed, was one of the best known landmarks of destruction. In the centre, they pointed out the National Library, shelled and burned along with much of the country's historical and literary treasures inside.

Low-level buildings in the centre initially seemed remarkably unscathed. However, on closer inspection I could see walls pockmarked with bullet holes and dented sidewalks, mini craters left behind by shells that had exploded. Plastic, the United Nations' UNHCR logo visible on it, covered many windows whose glass had shattered in the war and still had not been repaired.

We drove to the office, centrally located by a bridge over the Miljacka River, and parked in a lot full of four-wheel-drive Land Cruisers. I met more new colleagues – foreign delegates, most of them from European countries, and local employees, mainly Bosniac. I liked the bustle and sense of purpose in the office. No one sat idle. After introductions and a tour of each division, one colleague drove me to my new home, a ground-floor apartment near a park. The office had planned my arrival so well there seemed little left to do. I unpacked my suitcases and explored the apartment, which was large and dark. A bullet had grazed the living room ceiling, but all the walls remained intact. I had noticed many damaged tower blocks, with plastic sheeting where walls should be.

Across the street, a well-worn path led across a park. People walked along the path, so it seemed safe to follow behind. Soon dogs appeared, only a few at first, then a pack, one Great Dane and several other purebreds and mongrels of different sizes. Charlotte had said that many families turned their pets loose to fend for themselves when food ran short during the war. These dogs wagged their tails and seemed friendly. I wanted to pat them but kept my distance just in case. I heard that some still ran wild and attacked people.

I strolled through the city, past mosques, more parks and cafés. Then I wandered down to the river and along the embankment that led to the old town, which was peaceful and quite prosperous. I was unable to shake old Eastern Bloc travel habits, so my suitcases contained a stock of shampoo, soap, dried food and other basic supplies. But commerce appeared more advanced here just one and a half years since the war than in Ukraine six years after the collapse of Communism.

So much in Sarajevo seemed normal, but I found it impossible to forget the war for long. Hardly any trees remained in the city. I mostly saw stumps. Charlotte had described how people had chopped them down for firewood during the siege. Lost in thought, unable to really imagine siege-time Sarajevo, I wandered into a narrow alley, drawn by the mellifluous call to prayer that echoed off buildings and the soft light of a soon-to-set sun. Then I saw graffiti, the words scrawled in English on two walls: "Welcome to Hell" and "Paradise Lost."

The next morning when I arrived at work, I saw one of my new colleagues from the press office, Senad, on a sofa in the hallway, the morning papers spread before him. He was slightly younger than me and wore jeans and a blue blazer. Old World manners prevailed. He rose with a formal greeting, invited me to join him for coffee, returned with two cups of espresso and sank back into the sofa. I sat down beside him.

I glanced at the papers and noticed some printed in Cyrillic and others in the Roman alphabet.

"Our language split during the war," Senad told me. "We used to all speak Serbo-Croat. Now the Serbs speak Serb." He pointed to the paper printed in Cyrillic. "The Croats speak Croatian and we speak Bosnian. They're really all the same language, just a few different words in each, like dialects. But some people get upset if you say that."

"Were you born in Sarajevo?" I asked.

"I was. This beautiful city is my home." I told Senad about my walk the day before, my early impressions of the city and asked how long he had worked in the press office.

"I've been here the longest," he told me. I was surprised by his answer. Our three other colleagues were older and I had assumed that age translated into more years' service.

"Drago used to be on TV," Senad said. "Everyone remembers him from before the war. They love him because he reminds them of happier times. He can travel wherever he likes." As we talked more, Senad told me that even though the Dayton Peace Accord technically unified Bosnia and Herzegovina, a boundary line – an unofficial border – still existed between the Serb part of Bosnia and Herzegovina (Republika Srpksa) and the Muslim-Croat part (the Federation of Bosnia and Herzegovina), which included Sarajevo.

"Sooosan, I must tell you something," Senad said. "I will never cross that line." An awkward moment – I did not know what to say. Part of our job was to help promote unity by crossing that line as if it did not exist, to work with local offices across the country, helping people, especially the elderly whose families had emigrated during the war while they remained behind either because they could not or would not go.

"Drago will go with you when you visit the other side." As Senad drank his coffee, I could not help but notice that his hand shook.

During my first week in Sarajevo, few people that I met wanted to talk about the war. When information about their personal lives slipped out, I understood why. One woman saw her fiancé shot on the street by a sniper. Another took the garbage out one morning and found dead people stuffed in the bins. These images lingered during days when I was otherwise occupied with practical tasks. I took fieldwork tests for driver safety and radio operation. I learned the language of Alpha, Tango, Bravo, which was used for transmitting messages over the Land Cruiser radio and hovered somewhere between peace and conflict, never allowed to travel alone on the roads, always tethered to headquarters through mandatory radio contact at points along designated travel routes. Failure to check in could mean dispatch of a search crew.

"Never step off paved surfaces," my instructor said. I lost count of the number of times I had received this warning.

Having always been responsible for my own security and well-being before, I chafed under these rules but also craved them. In some part of my brain, I kept track of risks I had taken in the past in Chechnya, Moldova and Tajikistan and had begun to fear that my luck would soon run out. With rules like these in place in Sarajevo, that seemed unlikely. But when I learned all delegates had to request permission for leave outside the city on time off, I began to feel as though I had joined an army and signed my freedom away.

Sarajevo bristled with international peacekeepers and their hardware. Even a four-wheel-drive Land Cruiser seemed dwarfed by the large armoured vehicles that pulled up along-side at traffic lights. This military presence was so orderly – a world away from bullets fired in the air in Chechnya, Cossacks and their vodka in Trans Dniestria, and all those Kalashnikov-toting citizens. I saw none of that here. Rather I saw people going about their day-to-day business, cafés, full and shops, busy. Even if people were still armed, and rumours persisted of a country awash in guns, they kept their weapons out of sight.

I tried to describe these early impressions of Sarajevo to Sydney during our evening phone calls.

"So you mean there are guns and we could be shot?" he asked me one night.

"No, we'll be fine. It's perfectly safe here," I replied.

As Sydney's departure date for Sarajevo drew closer, he had trouble sleeping. I thrived in environments like this but wondered how he would adapt.

Just as Sydney was about to depart for Sarajevo, the arrests of people charged with war crimes began. Peacekeepers, SFOR (the NATO-led Stabilization Force), acted on two sealed indictments from the International Criminal Tribunal in the Hague. Indictments were kept secret — the number of them and when and how they would be acted on, all confidential information. I spent no time on political analysis. I only thought of complications to my personal life. Why did this have to happen now, so soon before Sydney would board his flight?

The arrests — both men lived in Republika Srpska — did not go well. Peacekeepers successfully captured one man but killed the other. Our security division pulled all foreign staff out of Republika Srpska and curtailed travel to minimize the risk of a retaliatory attack. I wrestled uncomfortably with the realization that even though as aid workers we were meant to be neutral, few perceived us this way.

The security division billeted a German delegate from Republika Srpska with me.

"They're throwing rocks at some foreigners," she told me over dinner that night.

"Sometimes they just shake their fists when we drive by. It'll pass, but it's not comfortable for us there now."

After dinner we listened to the news. The Sarajevo airport, where Sydney was supposed to land, had been closed. The Americans worried about the possibility of a rocket-launcher attack. All this was reported on the BBC. Sydney must know by now. I did not think he would take the news as calmly as the German delegate, with a shrug that this would all pass. I braced myself when the phone rang.

"My computer?" he said. I wasn't sure what he meant and wondered why he hadn't asked about the airport.

"Your computer?"

"I'm bringing it. It might be hard to get a good one there. Will I have trouble at customs? Can you arrange the paperwork?" We discussed the pros and cons of shipping one in. I promised to double-check with our office administrator. We chit-chatted about friends and Sydney's goodbye party in London. He told me he felt nervous and still couldn't sleep. I realized that Sydney didn't know about the airport closure and decided it was best not to contribute to his jitters. I kept quiet and felt consumed by guilt after we said goodbye.

Early the next day, Sydney called from Vienna to say that his connecting flight to Sarajevo had been cancelled.

"It's apparently really foggy at the Sarajevo airport and the plane can't land," he explained. I looked out the window and saw blue sky and sunshine. I said nothing.

A few hours later, we received a bulletin from security that the airport had re-opened. Not long after Sydney called.

"The fog's lifted," he said. "We'll board in a few minutes." He sounded excited, as was I.

A colleague helped shepherd Sydney's computer through customs. He beamed when it arrived in the passenger lounge. Our colleague drove us home via a back route, past neighbourhoods she knew well, apartment blocks with back halves sheared off, debris still visible from corridors that opened to the sky. These buildings lay along the wartime front line. She told us that some families had escaped before Serb paramilitary units arrived but some didn't. We drove by a gas pump still cordoned off with mine tape and veered around large potholes. We saw few people on the street. Sydney recorded these scenes on his video camera. Before we reached home, I told him why the airport had been closed. Safely here, now secure, he shrugged it off.

Sydney and I often explored Sarajevo on foot. We wandered up steep hills and looked down on the valley below. The city centre stretched out along the banks of the Miljacka River. Minarets poked high above sloping terracotta-tiled roofs against a backdrop of rounded mountaintops. On other days we wandered through former front-line neighbourhoods, properties still strewn with rubble, mine tape everywhere.

So many people had been internally displaced during the war. Serbs in Sarajevo went to Republika Srpska; Muslims from Serb areas flocked into the city and other nearby towns; many Croats settled in Croatia. We passed by semi-collapsed apartment blocks now occupied by refugees and saw small mountains of garbage piled up outside the buildings. The occupants tossed empty food tins, potato peelings and glass bottles out the windows. Worried there might be rats in the garbage, we stood far away. These piles concealed another potential danger. Mines sometimes lay in land underneath. The garbage made it hard for crews to find the mines and clear the land.

We both grew accustomed to security alerts, but I remained wary of mines. I acquired facts about them through work. There were about a million scattered around Bosnia-Herzegovina, not as many as in Cambodia and Afghanistan, but the situation here was uniquely perilous, because cities were mined.

One afternoon we walked through the outskirts of Sarajevo past whitewashed houses with rust-coloured roofs so steeply sloped they looked like ski chalets. Children stood on wrought-iron balconies. They called out to us and we waved back. Gardens grew larger, and space between the houses, more spacious. We passed piles of bricks, not rubble, but neat collections and soon saw the source: stripped structures, once houses. All that remained of one was cement pillars – a few bricks still clung in small arches where the pillars joined the base of the house, perhaps for extra reinforcement so the structure did not collapse – and a cement frame that showed how the rooms had been divided. Next door stood a one-storey wreck, somewhat less looted. Beside that, an elderly couple loitered in front of a well-preserved house separated from the sidewalk by reams of mine tape. The woman looked wistfully at the front door.

We stopped to chat in pidgin Bosnian and learned that the elderly couple stood in front of their own home.

"The house is mined," the man said. "We don't know when they'll be able to clear it."

"Where do you live now?" I asked.

"In the garage," the man said. "It wasn't mined, but it'll be cold in there in the winter. We have no heat." He explained some of this through mime.

I often saw demining crews and wondered what sort of person would choose this career and how crews accomplished their task with haphazard wartime front lines and few records to indicate where mines lay. For a while I did not worry. I took shortcuts and strolled across the lawn in front of a building where a friend worked. One day when I arrived, yellow tape fenced off the lawn. A crew worked behind the tape to extract a mine. As the months passed, statisticians compiled data. Mines had killed or injured about fifty to eighty people each month in Bosnia-Herzegovina.

On weekends, Sydney and I often crossed into Republika Srpska and walked with friends in the mountains above Pale, a town about fifteen kilometres southeast of Sarajevo; the terrain had been challenging enough for use in the 1984 winter Olympics. As we ascended in the Land Cruiser early one

Sunday from Sarajevo, mountain mist drifted across the road. It dulled all bright colours to a hazy, near uniform grey. We parked at the foot of the narrow stony road we would follow and saw the silhouettes of friends who had already arrived but not the mountains. They were shrouded in fog. Rocks covered part of the trail or spilled onto it from slopes nearby.

As the sun rose and the air warmed, the fog dissipated. I lagged behind with Gertrude, a new friend from Switzerland. Long shadows that stretched across straw-coloured grass and white rocks were our only company. When we paused during our conversation, we heard the crunch of gravel under our boots. The air was fresh, the sky a hopeful blue. I loved this peace and near solitude.

"We should move a bit faster now. I think we've fallen quite far behind," Gertrude said. I did not want to, but sensing her unease, I picked up my pace. We marched up the slope and soon saw others in the group. Their red, yellow and green jackets stood out like traffic lights. Close enough now, we relaxed our pace and drifted back into conversation.

Sometime later when we paused and noticed our surroundings again, we realized that Gertrude's friend Hans, who led the group, had veered off the path onto the scrubby hills and that we had followed. I stood still, imagining a mine under my feet. Then I ran.

"Wait," Gertrude shouted, but I did not stop until I reached Hans.

"We should get back onto the path. There could be mines," I said.

He laughed and said that he wanted to reach a bunker in the hills that had served as a military headquarters during the war. Then he walked away. The others followed. I did too, full of rage at myself for not going back but mostly rage directed at Hans, whose judgment I did not respect. If I was due for a brush with disaster, I did not want it to be that day, in the company of someone whom I now despised. As I trailed behind, silent and sullen at first, this dark mood passed as did my fear. I appreciated the barren beauty of the landscape and that first sense of freedom that came from walking again after so long across an open hillside, no pavement in sight. I had only been here for three months but realized much had changed already. For many years I had relied on my own judgment. Now, in Sarajevo, I learned to obey rules, even when I did not want to. But it felt good to take a risk again.

Near the end of August, not long after our walk in the hills above Pale, I drove to an event in Brčko, a city in a volatile, independent region of the country that linked the western and eastern parts of Republika Srpska, in northern Bosnia. I travelled with an American photographer named Louise. She would photograph the handover of vehicles from one of the international organizations to a local aid group. I was to participate in the ceremony. We meandered through the countryside, up steep hills covered in dense coniferous forests, the scent of pine wafting in when we rolled the windows down, along the banks of rushing rivers, whitecaps frothy, pools deep and aqua blue in more tranquil waters. It was always shocking when we rounded a bend and drove past the carcasses of burned-out houses in villages along the way. I diligently made radio contact with headquarters at each designated checkpoint. The farther into the countryside we travelled, the more troublesome this became. Soon we heard nothing but crackles. About halfway to Brčko we stopped near a bridge and persisted until finally a faint response came back.

"I'll move forward to a new position and try again in a minute," I shouted down the receiver. We climbed back into the Land Cruiser and rolled forward to an open space, where we hoped reception would improve. I heard a message with our call number and answered back. It was a colleague en route to the same event.

"Don't go to Brčko if you can't make it there by two o'clock," she shouted.

"What! Why not? The ceremony doesn't begin until three-thirty" I shouted back.

"It's starting early. Just turn back if you can't make it by two."

Louise and I consulted and decided we would continue. I pressed on the accelerator and did not slow down until half an hour later when we passed a long convoy of SFOR vehicles, mostly very large, pulled onto the shoulder of the road. As we approached the last one, we saw many men in uniform, who stood in an orderly line that stretched along the edge of the road in front of the vehicles. Their backs faced passing traffic as they answered the call of nature in unison, obedient to mine rules that kept them all on the asphalt.

We arrived in Brčko fifteen minutes after the event ended. I slumped over the wheel, tired and frustrated at this failure, irritated at the change in plan and bizarre speed of it all. I had attended similar events and none had proceeded like this. Just as we wondered what to do, a convoy of cars from the event drove past. A colleague recognized us and stopped the convoy. Delighted to find a photographer on board, he took us all back to the event site for a photo shoot. Then everyone else boarded cars and left Brčko immediately. We promised that we would too after we ate lunch.

The city felt strangely deserted. Many shops and restaurants had closed even though it was only mid-afternoon. We found one place open near the local UN office. As we ate, we noticed stalls where vendors sold CDs.

"It's my birthday," Louise said.

"Well, I know just the present for you."

We paid the bill and crossed over to the CD stalls. As we browsed, a blue truck nearly as long as the UN office parked directly in front of us. It shielded the building and blocked our access to the street.

"This is a little strange," Louise said.

"Weird. We're totally boxed in. This isn't great for me. I'm claustrophobic."

Louise selected her present, a CD titled "Girl Power." I bought it, then we walked to the end of the truck. In the open back, we saw concrete barricades piled inside.

I heard the crackle of the radio, the call number for our Land Cruiser and ran to answer it, but the dispatcher couldn't hear me call back.

"We'd better go," I said to Louise.

"I wonder what's going on?"

"I'd like to find out, but you know how it is – an order's an order. We were supposed to be gone by two."

At the junction that led to a big market, the Arizona, near Brčko, we heard the radio crackle again. I pulled into the market and radioed back.

"Have you left Brčko?" the dispatcher asked.

"Yes, we're on our way back. What's going on?" I received no information, just call-in instructions for the next designated checkpoint.

"How about a quick look around since we're here?" I asked Louise. I had heard about the Arizona, set up for free trade but better known as a smuggling centre. We got out and wandered around the stalls — tabletops that teemed with cigarette cartons, CDs or liquor, makeshift canvas awnings that looked like sides of dismantled tents held up by warped wooden poles. The whole place had the ramshackle yet permanent look of a squatters' camp. I suspected the arms that I had heard were for sale lay under sacks at the back. This strangely deserted place gave me the shivers. I wanted to leave. We reached Tuzla before dark, where we celebrated Louise's birthday and spent the night with colleagues.

The next morning we heard that SFOR had deployed troops across the northeast. A local Serb leader tried to take over police stations and a television transmitter. Hundreds of SFOR Soldiers now patrolled the streets. In Brčko, shooting incidents occurred. All that tension made sense now.

At 9:30 a.m. we left for Sarajevo. SFOR helicopters circled overhead. We passed SFOR tanks on the road. They travelled toward Republika Srpska. As we drove south, this commotion receded. We wound our way along curvy mountain roads, veered onto the wrong side when our lane became blocked by boulders that had fallen from the steep mountainsides above and held our breath that we would not collide with oncoming traffic as we rounded a sharp bend, still forced onto the wrong side of the road. When we arrived in Sarajevo, I dropped Louise at her house and then drove to the office.

That evening I tuned into the BBC news to discover there was more trouble in Brčko. SFOR had used tear gas to disperse a crowd of about a thousand, one American soldier had been injured, and SFOR had evacuated unarmed UN police. A BBC reporter described an attack by a crowd on a bridge that led from Brčko into Croatia. One person had grabbed her microphone; a woman in the crowd had whacked the reporter across her legs with a wooden board. Then others joined in. Soldiers dragged the reporter to safety in a SFOR house. I thought of all the planks of wood in Grozny and Moldova, remembered my own microphone from radio days and felt grateful for the orders that had gotten me out of Brčko in time.

We organized many events for children or the elderly affected by war. Our office helped arrange a picnic for pensioners from Goražde, a city so badly damaged that it looked as though fighters had extracted vengeance from the buildings as well as the people. Shells had blown the roofs off many houses. Birds nested in holes in the walls. Almost no structure remained intact. Our organization financed mobile teams to patch houses, but some were so badly destroyed that they remained beyond repair. A lot of people relied on charity for a place to live. For many, this picnic was their first trip to the countryside in six years.

I drove five kilometres to the picnic site, past more destruction, over a bridge and down a riverbank; most of the countryside was mined. A windy road, little more than a muddy bog, led to the site, which was situated on a safe patch of land.

I worked with colleagues. We stretched a long blanket out in a clearing by the riverbank. Men sliced lamb on a tree stump. We placed it on plates with cheese, bread and vegetables. "This'll be the first meat for them in a long time," a colleague from Goražde said.

Soon more colleagues arrived with pensioners. We helped them down to the blanket. They ringed the edge of it and grew excited by all the food. Some people did not have strong enough teeth to chew the meat, no matter how finely we cut it. When they had finished their meals, the pensioners lingered in the warm summer sun, watched bathers splash in the river, made new friends, gossiped and marvelled at the beauty of the countryside. My throat felt tight — it took so little to make them happy. One man described how grenades had blown up members of his family. A son survived. He lived in Sarajevo and could not afford the bus fare to visit Goražde. When we had to go, no one wanted to leave.

I drove three picnickers home, a couple and a single woman. The couple lived in a house, damaged but still habitable; the woman, in a refugee centre located in the front wing of the local elementary school. When we reached the centre, a little girl in a crumpled, dusty dress, her face smeared with dirt, approached us. A beggar, I thought at first, but the woman whom I had driven home introduced me to seven-year-old Alicia and told me that she lived in the centre with her mute mother. Alicia was so excited to meet a foreigner that she insisted on giving me a tour. It was hard not to feel depressed as I walked through the doors.

Alicia and her mother lived in the gymnasium with the other refugees. Each had a single wooden bed; twenty-three ringed the gymnasium wall. Ragged bundles of belongings stacked on top of one another stood alongside the beds. Beside, on the floor, lay plates of leftover macaroni. An old man, still in bed, beckoned me over.

I introduced myself.

"A pleasure to make your acquaintance," he said. "May I make a request through you?" he asked.

"Certainly," I said.

"Now this is a request, not a complaint," he insisted. "We're grateful for the food, but potatoes and macaroni day after day, it's a bit monotonous. Could we have something different to eat?" Alicia tugged my hand. She wanted to continue the tour. I told the man I would inquire on his behalf.

"How long have you lived here?" I asked Alicia as she skipped along beside me across the gymnasium floor.

"Five years," she said. So she moved here as a toddler. She had really known no other home.

She showed me a classroom that looked like a dormitory. I smelled fresh paint. I asked a workman about the gym accommodation.

"Temporary," he said, "just till we've painted here. This one's for the men."

"Come see where my mother and I sleep," Alicia said. She hopped toward the classroom next door. I followed her into a cluttered hallway. Shards of glass lay scattered across the floor. In the bathroom, I tested the faucet. Only cold water trickled out, the basin was ringed with grime, the floor coated in dirt. Everything was scaled to a child's size. Elderly residents had to stoop down to use basins designed for people about four feet tall.

Not all the elderly were as vulnerable. Soon after I had toured the refugee centre, Louise and I visited a beneficiary whose house had been repaired by one of the mobile teams. We travelled from Sarajevo through villages, along secondary roads. These deteriorated into trails and two kilometres from our destination became impassable ruts. Louise and I parked the Land Cruiser, loaded provisions for the woman we would visit into backpacks and hiked a trail up the mountain through pine forest, fallen needles underfoot, all sounds hushed. Soon we reached a small house in a clearing. We stopped for directions, and as we made inquiries, a small woman with the shrivelled face of an apple doll appeared. I guessed that she was in her late seventies.

"Here I am," she said. She introduced herself as Božena and grinned a partially toothless grin. "You missed the turn. Follow me." At least, this is what I thought she said. She bounded down the path, headscarf flapping, skirt swooshing. We straggled behind, our relative youth put to shame by this geriatric dynamo.

Božena turned onto a barely visible path that branched off from the main trail. We walked a short distance and then reached her house. A colleague from a local organization who spoke both languages had already arrived and translated for us.

"She wants to show you her house," our colleague said. Božena pointed out restored walls; new glass panes filled the window frames. We saw patches on the roof. All this work had been done by our mobile teams. Božena clasped her hands together as if in prayer.

Now that it had been repaired, her house looked inviting. Fire burned in a cast-iron stove, smoke puffed out the chimney. We complimented Božena on her lovely home. She beamed again and then led us to the garden.

"She says she wants to show you where she slept during the war," our colleague told us.

"Was there actually fighting here?" I asked. Our colleague translated, waited for a reply and then said, "none here, though you can see the damage from what happened close by. A group of soldiers came once. She was in the forest and heard them before she reached home, so she hid until they left. They took all the food. After that she wouldn't sleep in the house, because she was afraid they might come back."

I saw a vegetable patch in the garden and scrubby ground behind. We walked beyond this and through tall grass that concealed a small door in a hillock. Božena opened the door. We peered at a dark space not even big enough for a coffin.

"She slept here?" Božena nodded and mimed how she curled up in a ball to fit inside.

"Even in winter?" Božena nodded vigorously and held up two fingers.

"Through two winters?" More translation and then vigorous nodding. That a woman in her seventies had physically survived such conditions seemed remarkable, but to psychologically survive and emerge cheerful spoke of even greater strength. When I grew old, I wanted to be like that.

The hills that ringed Sarajevo and towns nearby were always a draw. Work often took me into remote mountainous regions. In our free time, Sydney and I also ventured out into them. On most winter weekends we skied near Pale, in Republika Srpska, which was a short drive from Sarajevo and close to paths where we had walked the summer before. Sydney had a job now. Our circle of friends had expanded to include some of his colleagues. We often had their company on the hills. A popular weekend ski spot before the war for Sarajevans, few crossed the line now to ski here again.

We drove up in the Land Cruiser, four-wheel drive engaged, sometimes still sliding backwards and sideways down icy roads near the resort. On those occasions, I pumped on breaks that did not even help slow us down. The Land Cruiser would stop with a gentle thud when we hit a snowbank. Men always appeared from somewhere and helped push us back on the road; we reciprocated when we passed others in the same predicament. There was no automobile association but we could always count on help from strangers. Old World courtesy prevailed even after all the atrocities of war.

Despite economic deprivations, the resort maintained its own dated charm. The dining room had wood panelling and wood chairs. The waitresses were sometimes surly, sometimes not. The restaurant was never full, so we could always linger over lunch. The resort had a pool, which was almost as much an attraction for me as the hills. Sometimes after lunch I stayed indoors for a swim, though it took courage to jump into the pool. A tall windowed wall along one side of the pool deck looked out onto a snowy landscape dotted with pine trees. The pool water was as cold as snow. There was no evidence of any heater that worked, but I loved to swim and after several minutes always managed to take the plunge. My breath was taken away by the iciness of the water, but I always felt happy to swim again.

Sydney preferred the hills. We would ski together in the morning, separate after lunch and then meet at the end of the day, return our tall, thin rental skis, then drive back down into Sarajevo to meet friends for dinner and relax before the work week began again. I missed the freedom of journalism but slowly acclimatized to office life and enjoyed the company of new colleagues, especially on road trips, when there was time for more than office talk and a chance to get to know one another.

In the spring Senad and I travelled to Switzerland for a workshop. We took a taxi together to the Sarajevo airport, past those devastated neighbourhoods swaddled in mine tape.

"I served there," Senad said. He had never spoken of his war experiences.

"It's hard to believe that anyone ever lived in those houses or walked along those streets," I replied.

"Sooosan, what hell."

Once we were settled in the departure lounge, Senad talked non-stop. His memories of war had been triggered. A student, not a soldier when the fighting began, he had the disposition of a thoughtful academic, not someone inclined toward the military.

"My parents, even I, did not think it would be possible for neighbours to turn against neighbours," he said. "We watched the Serbs gather on the hilltops, we saw the guns pulled into place, but we still didn't believe they would shoot at us."

"And . . ." I prompted.

"Even when we heard the first shots, my parents and I still sat in our living room. Then it started to get really bad and we went down to the basement," he said.

"After a few weeks, I couldn't stand it. I couldn't take it any longer, waiting for them to arrive, to smash in the door of our house, to kill us." Senad decided to leave home and join the fighters.

"Anything was better than just to sit there, waiting," he said. I listened as he described the informal militia set up to defend the city, how he walked to join his unit and dodged snipers along the way. I had so many questions but did not want to interrupt this unburdening, so I just stayed quiet.

He described the area where he fought as one half controlled by Bosniacs, the other half, by Serbs. The front line was a main street that separated the two sides.

"Sometimes we had to drive along that road to move supplies and people," Senad said.

"How dangerous was it?" I asked.

"Most of the time we waited," he said. "It was boring but not a usual boredom. There was so much tension." I thought of how his hands shook each morning as he held his coffee, and now suspected that his nerves were frayed as a result of his wartime experience.

"Snipers fired from both sides. You never knew when there would be an attack."

"Were you involved in a lot of fighting?" I asked. He drew a breath and told me about his worst day in Dobrinje, a day of deliveries when he had to drive down the front line in a van.

"We drove really fast, and zigzagged to make sure the snipers couldn't get us," Senad said. "Our tire burst," he said. "The driver lost control. We didn't know if a sniper had hit the tire, if we'd run over something jagged or if the tire was just weak and had blown on its own." He described how the van flipped and landed on its side, leaving Senad and his friends, who sat in the cargo section in the back, banged up and dazed. That part of the van had no windows.

"We just sat there in the dark," he said. "So much dust swirled in the air, I couldn't breathe. I thought I'd suffocate or choke to death." Senad and his friends heard a click of the ignition, an engine that stalled, curses from the driver. Stuck in a wreck in no man's land along the front line, they discussed their odds of survival and what to do.

"Either we could sit there and wait for them to open fire, shell us, lob grenades, or we could get out and run," Senad said.

"It seemed an eternity, but maybe it was only a few minutes. We all agreed. No one wanted to wait for slaughter. We forced a door open. I remember the sun was so bright. We all got out and we ran. Thanks to God that we all made it alive," he said. He spoke more of life on the front line, friendships formed there, classes missed, a sense of falling behind, lost opportunity.

"When peace came, I was so glad that my family and I lived, but the war cheated me of time," he said. I hesitated to ask one question because it was intrusive, but asked it anyhow.

"How did it feel the first time you shot someone?"

"Sooosan, I never shot anyone. I always just fired at bushes. If I thought that I had killed someone, I would want to kill myself." Such destruction in that neighbourhood – I could not believe that a soldier who served there would never have to shoot to kill, even if only in self-defence. I wondered if Senad's mind was playing tricks on him and suppressing bad memories.

I know mine had. I told Senad how I had recently reread a diary entry about a road trip that Sydney and I had taken the summer before, not long after we arrived in Sarajevo and how shocked I had been to find out that I had completely blocked out one event that I recorded in my diary.

That entry described a trip to Zagreb from Sarajevo – Sydney, a friend and I travelled in the Land Cruiser. The drive was uneventful until we neared Bihać. On our approach, we rounded the beginning of a bend, a long, steep curve down a mountainside, stopped suddenly by half a dozen stationary cars on the road. Sydney and I rolled our windows down. We heard the most terrible wail. We got out of the Land Cruiser and ran down the road toward the person in distress.

"The first aid kit," I shouted at Sydney, who was tall and long-limbed and already far ahead of me. "I'll run back to get it." He stopped. I retrieved the kit from the Land Cruiser and gave it to him. He sprinted down the road; I followed but lagged behind.

I could no longer see Sydney by the time I reached the logs. At first I did not understand their significance, awed by their size, gargantuan pick-up sticks strewn across the road. No traffic could pass. The truck that carried them had skidded across the road and now lay on its side, partially wedged against the steep mountain cliff.

A man in his fifties wailed. I found his anguish harrowing but could not understand the source of it. He stood and had no visible injuries. The man grabbed the logs, held his head and paced back and forth desperately. It was devastating to watch him.

Sydney stood farther down the road by a police officer. He offered him the first aid kit. The police officer shook his head. What I wrote next I did not remember, though words in my diary, my handwriting, must be true.

The man who wailed bent down to pick an object up, a severed leg. He clutched the jean- and shoe-clad leg to his chest and then threw it back onto the ground, where a second severed leg lay. Horrified, I turned away. As I reread the entry in my diary describing this gruesome scene, I felt that I was reading an account of someone else's recollections and could not accept that I had witnessed this.

I remembered the scene I recorded in the next entry. Sydney approached me, his face blank; his body slightly hunched. He went to the side of the road and crouched down to vomit.

"Don't go any farther. There's an ugly sight, a squashed body," he said.

Our friend, who spoke fluent Croatian, remained near the other cars and spoke with drivers who knew what had happened. When we returned, he told us that the wailing man drove the truck, took the corner quickly and lost control. He and a passenger, his son, jumped from the cab while the truck was still moving. The father landed in bushes, his son was killed, trapped beneath the logs. I said to Senad that it seemed such an unfair fate – to survive the war and then die like that.

He said nothing in reply and just switched the topic of conversation to our workshop in Switzerland. Many of the sessions would focus on digital information. Senad and I would learn techniques to assist with one main focus of our work, transmitting information to Bosnian refugees living in countries like Germany and Norway that would help them decide whether or not to return home. So many refugees remained outside the country and so much of the population in Bosnia was internally displaced.

Louise and her husband Goran had also been affected by the war. Goran retained his family house throughout the war, though their summer house, about a forty-five-minute drive from Sarajevo, housed a family of Serbian refugees, displaced by fighting.

One morning in early June, Louise telephoned. "Guess what?" she said.

I could not guess her news.

"The Serb family at Goran's place is going home." Once this family left, Goran could reclaim his summer house. "Why don't you and Sydney come up for the weekend to help us celebrate?" I accepted the invitation.

Sydney drove. We left the outskirts of Sarajevo, passed a major SFOR base and soon turned onto narrow country roads. As we rounded the bend in one windy lane, we nearly ran into a large moving truck travelling in the opposite direction. Sydney reversed a long distance until he found a gap where he could pull over to let the truck pass. I felt relieved that he was driving, not me.

"Hi," Louise said with a smile when we finally pulled up to the front door of the country house. "Goran's in a bad mood. The movers dropped the fridge on his hand." A few minutes later, we heard footsteps on the stairs. Goran came into the kitchen, nursing his bandaged hand. He was shirtless because of the heat.

"*Zdravo* [hello]," he said to Sydney, waved at me, then turned toward Louise. As he moved, I saw his back, which shocked me far more than his injured hand. His back was covered in a tangle of thick, welted scars. Goran and Louise discussed the dinner menu, then Goran left. I said nothing but Louise must have sensed my shock and understood the cause.

"The war," she said.

"What happened?"

"He belonged to the White Swallows." I told Louise that I had not heard of them.

"They were an elite group of fighters. They tried to hold Mount Igman, key territory," she said.

"His unit was decimated. He was injured, still conscious, but he couldn't move. He watched his friends die. Then he just lay there and thought he'd die too." I pictured the scene as she described how rescuers had found Goran and carried him down the mountain, blood dripping from his body, all gashes and pulp.

"You'll never believe who operated on him and saved his life."

"Who?" I asked.

"His brother. He was the surgeon on duty that night."

Our topic of conversation changed as quickly as it had started. My mind raced to catch up, still dwelling on the battle scene, the aftermath. I wondered how Goran coped with all this. I could only relate through stories from World War II, but that was the past, the stuff of history books, not the present. Current events had so affected the lives of friends here.

The door opened again. A tall man holding an axe hobbled into the kitchen.

Louise introduced Sydney and me to Goran's friend Zoran. He had just chopped firewood and wondered if Louise and Goran wanted some.

"How perfect!" Louise said to him. "We'll use it for our barbecue tonight. Come join us." Zoran thanked Louise but said that he already had plans. He limped away. We heard the thud of wood as it landed on the verandah and the patter of rain on the rooftop.

"What happened to Zoran's foot?" I asked Louise.

"Half of it was blown off by a mine."

"That's terrible." Louise had warned of mine-infested land by Goran's country house. "Did it happen here?" I asked.

"Oh, no, when he was with his unit just toward the end of the war and he was really lucky."

"Lucky?"

"His unit walked through a field. No one knew it was mined. When they marched back, Zoran stepped on a mine at the edge of the field. He fell forward into a clear area. If he had fallen back, his injuries would have been much worse."

As we washed mushrooms and peppers, Louise told Sydney and me more about Zoran. He could not find a comfortable prosthesis. With no clinic in Sarajevo, Zoran had to order models from Germany and various other countries, but none fit properly.

"What a bad time, such pain," Louise said. "Everything chafed." Then Zoran found an American doctor online. They corresponded. The doctor sent him another model, which still didn't quite fit right. But Zoran was skilled with his hands and modified this prosthesis, in consultation with the doctor, for a snug fit and minimal discomfort.

Through the window we saw the rain stop, the sky dramatic now, half dark with thunderclouds, half brilliant blue.

"Let's pick some plums while we have the chance," Louise said. Sydney, meat cleaver in hand, stayed behind in the kitchen. Louise and I stepped out the front door and walked down to the orchard, hung heavy with purple fruit. Louise turned up the bottom of her T-shirt, held it in one hand, stretched high and picked fruit with the other, the plums nestled in a pile in her makeshift basket. I copied her.

As we moved down the orchard rows, a reminder from Louise: "It's fine to walk here, but some of the fields are mined."

In the house, we transferred our harvest to a basket. Sydney's pile of meat grew taller, a wooden bowl brimmed with salad, bright peppers lined a tray, ready for the barbecue. As the sun fell lower in the sky, mist rose up. We heard the dog bark and saw him amble up the road with Goran, who clutched a bottle. When he entered the kitchen, he held the bottle high, like a trophy.

"*Šljivovica*," he said. "The neighbours make it. They have the best plums." He'd already sampled the brew.

"We can watch the sun set from the balcony," Louise said. "The view over the hills is beautiful. Let's go up." Goran led us through empty rooms. Furniture lay in a jumbled pile in one room, untouched since the movers had arrived that morning. A boom box stood by the balcony. Louise put on a CD. I recognized it as ambient electronica but did not know the group.

"Fabulous," Sydney said. "I have this one."

Goran found chairs. We sampled the *šlivovica*, then toasted the summer house, Goran and Louise, and the fragile peace. I stood up for a better view. Louise and Sydney joined me. I commented on the bucolic scene stretched out below, green rolling hills dotted with small houses, earth churned up in one field on a hillside.

"That's great, I guess they're farming again," I said.

"What do you mean?" Louise asked.

"There, on the hillside, that dug-up earth. Farmers must be planting crops."

"Oh, that's not a field," Louise said. "It's a mass grave, an exhumation." I listened, horrified, as she told me – her tone, matter-of-fact – that Serbs had marched Bosniacs who lived in the area over the ridge, shot some – possibly one hundred – and dumped their bodies in that grave. I wondered what wartime nightmares Louise and Goran had experienced that rendered a mass grave commonplace and accepted as an unremarkable part of the landscape.

I wanted to move away. It felt indecent to gaze at a grave like that. We went downstairs, the air on the ground-floor verandah redolent with the smoky smell of meat that roasted. Goran stood over the barbecue; flames leaped up through the grill, bright orange in the dark. He tended kebabs and peppers, turned them regularly, fat sizzled as it hit the fire. Sydney poured more slivovic, then wine. We toasted Goran's neighbours, his newly reclaimed house. His dog joined us. He soon lay tucked under the table, ready for scraps to fall. Music wafted down from the balcony. Platters that spilled over with meat and vegetables filled the table. Slowly the fire died down.

Sydney left the table, slid away in the dark. A few minutes later, he returned to his seat and calmly said, "I've chopped my thumb off." Louise and I both thought that Sydney meant that he had cut his thumb. Louise handed him a roll of army gauze, which she still had in her pocket from Goran's accident earlier in the day. I could not see Sydney for lack of light but wondered at his tone of voice. I walked over to his chair.

"I've got to find my thumb," he muttered. By now his hand was well bandaged. I told him not to stand. He said that he had accidentally cut part of his thumb off while chopping wood at the side of the house. I ran around there; the dog followed, sniffing the ground. He was a Doberman, the one breed that I feared. I pushed the dog away, still a race between us for the thumb.

Louise arrived with a flashlight and held the dog back. I found the thumb. The dog strained under Louise's grip. She shone the flashlight my way and I felt pleased to see that I held only a small bit of thumb – about half the nail but fortunately cut on a diagonal so that less thumb behind it was gone. Louise held a teacup with cold water. We did not know what to do but put the thumb bit in it.

We returned to the verandah. Sydney sat on a sofa, his head bent low. He said that he felt ill. Louise ran to the kitchen for a bowl; I rushed over to the Land Cruiser so that I could reverse it and face the right direction for the road so that it was ready to depart for the hospital. It was dark and the clearing where the Land Cruiser stood was very small, with a ridge nearby. Unfamiliar with the terrain and hardly able to see, I manoeuvred the Land Cruiser so that it hung over the ridge. I stopped, worried that I might plunge down into the field below, where Louise had warned me not to walk. I shouted. Goran ran out of the house. He directed me back onto flat ground. I shook as we bundled Sydney on board and left for Sarajevo. Sydney sat quietly in the back.

"My thumb throbs," he said.

"Just scream," Louise told him. "That's the best way to manage pain."

"It's not in my nature," Sydney replied. I could see in the rear-view mirror that he sat quietly, hunched forwards, head bowed. I headed for the hospital on the SFOR base.

When we arrived at the base gate, Louise rolled down her window and shouted, "Can somebody help us here? We have an emergency." The guard, startled, I think, by Louise's take-charge attitude, opened the barrier and waved us through.

We saw Jeeps and soldiers everywhere and heard helicopters that hovered in the darkness somewhere nearby. Medical personnel ran from a building, and surrounded the Land Cruiser.

"Can he walk?" one man asked us. Sydney mumbled that he could. Medics led us into an emergency room. A tall, broad-shouldered German doctor, who spoke flawless English, tended to Sydney immediately. The doctor told us the thumb bit could not be reattached.

"The wound is good, clean," he added. He said that he would graft it with artificial skin.

"Did we do the right thing with the thumb bit?" I asked. The doctor described immersion in water as a mistake. "Don't worry, though, it was too small to be reattached," he added, whether out of kindness only or clinical truth I did not know.

Goran picked Louise up. I stayed with Sydney in Emergency. He lay on a medical bench that resembled a narrow operating table. I sat in a chair nearby. The doctor said that he would change the dressing on Sydney's thumb and clean the wound. He left for a while. When he came back, he pulled curtains around the medical bench. Sydney's feet poked out from under the curtain because he was tall.

I heard a sharp intake of breath from Sydney as the doctor worked. Then I saw his feet arch up in pain. I wanted to pull the curtains back and comfort him but knew that I could do nothing. Then Sydney's feet went limp. What had happened? I heard the doctor calmly say, "Sydney, open your eyes. Can you hear me, Sydney?" Then medics rushed past with a large machine. I heard beeps and other noises, then saw Sydney's feet move. A few minutes later the doctor parted the curtains.

"I'm sure you're wondering what happened," he said. I was.

The doctor said that Sydney had reacted badly to the anesthetic, lost consciousness and stopped breathing, so he was put on a respirator. I wanted to see him. Medical staff wheeled Sydney out on a stretcher. He looked dead or if not, then close to it. The tears that ran down the side of his face were the only sign of life. He stared up at the ceiling, his pupils the size of pinholes, and did not respond to stimulation. I felt shocked and could not speak.

"Don't worry. He looks much worse than he is," the doctor said.

In a daze, I followed the stretcher to the intensive care unit. I wondered about brain damage. An orderly stopped me just inside the entrance. The medical team wheeled Sydney away. The orderly gave me a surgical gown and slippers to put on. Soon the doctor returned.

"He's talking nonsense," he said. "Would you like to see him?" I nodded.

"Will he recover?" I asked.

"He should," the doctor said. Why not, "he will"? Why this qualifier? My heart beat faster. My body moved slower. The doctor led me down a corridor to a bed in a cubicle where Sydney lay.

I spoke softly, stroked his shoulder, told him what had happened. He understood but forgot within seconds. I explained once more. He forgot again.

Machines hummed, someone coughed in a cubicle nearby, Sydney slept. When he woke, he said that his face, which looked normal, felt strange.

Speaking very slowly he said, "My face . . . feels . . . like . . . the . . . Oslobodjenie building." I was so happy that he remembered Sarajevo's hallmark of destruction. I felt hopeful now that he would recover and explained once more what had happened. This time he remembered.

He rested again. As time passed, he spoke in full sentences. At first his thoughts were random thoughts, but then we were able to have short conversations. Then he started to laugh and said, "You have tentacles coming out of your head. You look like an octopus."

Delusions – what next? The doctor appeared. He examined Sydney, spoke with him and said that Sydney would be fine but that he could not explain the cause of his condition. I sat in the chair as Sydney rested. I thought of Goran and his scars, and wondered if this much can go wrong in peacetime, how bad had it been during the war?

The doctor returned and admitted Sydney to a ward for observation.

"He's fine," the doctor said. "We'll keep him here for some tests. Then he'll be able to go home."

A few days later I drove Sydney home from the hospital. As we climbed the steps to our apartment, we saw the neighbour's children and their uncle. It was nearly a year since we had arrived in Sarajevo and nearly a year since the children's father had died. Their uncle, remembering too, told us that their father's death had been the eleventh in the family in five years.

"Everyone else in the war. But my brother, this last one, it's not knowing what happened that's the worst."

I remembered the day well. Sydney and I had just arrived in Sarajevo. We had come home one day and noticed people milling around outside the neighbour's. Eventually we understood that someone had died, a grandparent, we both assumed.

"*Ne, otac*," a woman corrected. That word, close enough to the Russian – father. Young, forty-two years old, large, strong, so healthy, we did not understand how. We entered to pay our respects. People sat on sofas and chairs or stood. Everyone drank coffee. We were offered cups of it and joined the group.

A woman who spoke English explained that our neighbour, a bus driver on the Bosnia-Germany route, had been asked, at short notice, to take a tour group to Dubrovnik instead.

"Fate," she said. "His son heard the news on television, a report on the accident. They announced his name." Appalled that a five-year-old should learn of his father's death this way, I asked how he was.

"He and his mother are so traumatized they won't talk."

No one knew more than the information provided in the broadcast. The report said the bus had swerved several times on the steep coastal road near Dubrovnik and plunged over the edge – five people were dead, several more wounded. The accident had occurred at about 3 a.m. The bus was discovered the next morning. People at the gathering speculated that our neighbour had either fallen asleep while driving, had a heart attack or been forced to swerve to avoid a collision.

It was nice to see the children so happy now, wrestling on the ground. Sydney tickled them with his good hand, held his thickly bandaged thumb high so they would not accidentally bump it. We played for a while. We told their uncle that we would be leaving in a month, taking a holiday in Australia, Vietnam and Thailand and then returning to Canada.

"Home to be with family," he said. "That's where you belong." He watched as the little boy raced up and down the steps, his sister, shy in comparison, hovered near her uncle. I crouched down and asked her, "How old are you now?" even though I already knew that she was three. She held up the right number of fingers, which inadvertently made a Serb sign that her uncle despised.

"No, never like that," he said. He took her fingers and bent them back down. "Never ever hold your fingers up like that." Her face dropped. She knew that she had done something wrong but did not understand what. My feelings were as confused as hers. I felt sympathy for a man who had lost so many in the war but sadness also to see hatred passed from one generation to the next.

THE ORANGE
REVOLUTION

"It's dark," I said, "claustrophobic."

"Bad karma," Sydney replied.

We could have been discussing the state of our marriage, but really were talking about our new house in Toronto. Filled with buyer's remorse and gloomy thoughts, we sat at the kitchen table in August 2000, surrounded by boxes. The movers had just left. Our conversation ended. I turned my chair, looked out the glass door that faced the garden and thought about the change that lay ahead. On Monday I would start a new job in communications and begin a part-time MBA; work nine to five, study at night.

Soon, I had no time for reflection. On lecture days I woke, rushed to work, left at 5 p.m., grabbed a sandwich before class, returned home at 10:30 p.m., spent half an hour with Sydney, then we went to bed. Our lives drifted further apart. We occupied separate zones in our three-bedroom house. A programmer, he spent most of his time in the basement, immersed in his world of computers. I sprawled through rooms upstairs, scattering my books across various beds. Sydney set up a server. Now, even at home, we communicated mostly through email. We developed different circles of friends. The inevitable soon occurred and we separated. I left the house the weekend Sydney moved out. I did not want to witness the final moments of our life together, the end of our marriage.

I had scoffed at the idea of self-help books. Now a pile of them towered by my bed and I found solace between the covers. When I felt unexpectedly happy at work one day a few weeks after our separation, tears suddenly welled up in my eyes. I dove under my desk and told people who entered my cubicle that I was adjusting a network cable. I remained hidden until the tears stopped. I did not know how to manage this roller-coaster of emotions. The books said the emotions would subside. I didn't believe it but hoped the books were right.

Selling the house helped, as did old friendships. Marta had moved back to Canada. She was a professor at a university near Toronto. We moved in together. In the evenings, we slipped into the world of Kiev. Marta taught East European history and politics. She hosted literary circles at home. I would return after late-night MBA study groups, hear the sound of Ukrainian chatter in the kitchen and feel happy that I still remembered some of the language. Months passed quickly.

I graduated from the MBA program and started a new job in an investment advisory firm that had an alternative style of analysis. This job seemed a near perfect fit. It was international but based at home and involved travel. I liked my colleagues and my work.

Marta left for a sabbatical in Ukraine. I found a new apartment. Alone for the first time in many years, I felt strangely optimistic as my self-help books said the newly divorced sometimes did. I was happy to hang on to that feeling. I still had it in November 2004, when I first saw the massive street protests in Kiev on television.

"Quick, turn the TV on," I told my mother by phone. "You can almost see my old apartment in the background." She had visited Kiev in 1997 and quickly recognized the place, as amazed as I was by the huge number of people crammed into Independence Square, many dressed in orange.

"What's going on?" she asked. I wondered how to explain developments in Ukrainian politics since she had visited, especially as I did not fully understand them. A journalist named Georgiy Gongadze, who criticized the regime, had disappeared in 2000 and was presumed murdered. A presidential body-guard defected and released tapes that implicated the president, though nothing was ever fully investigated or proved. Protests built over four years. Then a rigged election triggered this huge protest. That much I could explain to my mother.

"The current president's term limit is up. He selected a suc-cessor candidate, Victor Yanukovych, and tried to rig the elec-tion so Yanukovych would win. When that was exposed, the protest began. All those people dressed in orange say the oppo-sition candidate, Victor Yushchenko, really won. The protesters are fed up. They say they're not going to accept corruption and abuse of power anymore."

"Those two Victors, their names sound a lot alike. It's con-fusing," she said. I agreed.

I missed Marta. She was still in Kiev, living in her apart-ment next door to my old place. We swapped messages. A net-work approached me to help cover the Orange Revolution. I told Marta.

"Come, you must!" she wrote back. I thought about it as I monitored newscasts at work.

"What's going on in Kiev?" my boss asked. He waved a newspaper with two pictures of Viktor Yushchenko, one marked "before" and one "after."

"I can't believe this. He was such a handsome guy, but this looks like Frankenstein," my boss said as his finger jabbed the "after" shot. "The report said someone poisoned him. I thought that only happened in the Middle Ages," he added. "I'm surprised they didn't just knock him off. What have you heard?"

I only knew what I read. The deputy director of the Ukrainian Security Services had invited Yushchenko for dinner. Soon after the dinner Yushchenko fell ill. His face erupted in large, blistery bumps. His body was wracked with pain, but he still campaigned, made speeches, soldiered on.

"Yes, well, sometimes Ukraine is a strange place," I replied, feeling oddly defensive of a country I thought of as an adopted homeland. "One state television report said Yushchenko looks like that because he has herpes; another blamed sushi."

"Sushi? You can't be serious." I had to nod yes, amazed, too, by such lies. Then I told him about the network coverage offer.

"How badly do you want to go?" I dithered and turned the offer down.

After work I took the subway to the west end of the city, where Ukrainian Canadians held a rally in favour of Viktor Yushchenko. I saw orange everywhere – balloons, T-shirts, flickering candle flames – and heard the soothing murmur of Ukrainian that I now heard nowhere else. A pro-Yushchenko poster hung on one of the consulate doors.

I could not concentrate at work the next day and was quiet in the car during the commute home with colleagues. Restless, I left my apartment and walked downtown, with no particular destination in mind, but my feet took me to a travel agent's office. Since I was there, I thought that I would ask about the price of flights to Kiev.

"It's the last day of a seat sale on Lufthansa," the agent told me.

I handed her my credit card and booked a non-refundable flight to Kiev.

At home, I panicked. Work deadlines loomed; I had not even formally requested time off.

"I won't miss any of my deadlines," I promised my boss the next day. He gave me permission to go.

I could not imagine being there and not reporting. I sent an email to the foreign news editor at the Sunday edition of my old newspaper, the *Independent*, and felt so excited when he replied and commissioned a feature. Signed on for Orange Revolution coverage, I telephoned Marta to let her know I would be leaving the next day.

"Stay with me," she said. No invitation could have made me happier.

Men with gold teeth slumped on chairs in the Frankfurt Airport departure lounge. Seated first on the plane, I saw them totter down the aisle, then collapse into seats behind mine; the scent of alcohol – vodka, I thought – still lingered where they had passed. They tried to order another round before the flight took off. I checked my watch. It was 9:30 a.m. Time peeled back fourteen years.

I ate every item the flight attendants offered me, asked for seconds and worried about when food would next be available. I knew this was irrational, but the feeling was too urgent to ignore. Full for now, I reclined my seat. I thought of my father. I would land in Kiev on his birthday. His death ten years earlier triggered my decision to leave Ukraine, make my way home and abandon journalism.

I thought again of advice from my friend Roma. I had confided in her that I still fought wanderlust.

"Maybe it's an addiction," I said.

"Stop relying on external stimulation! Find it from within," she insisted. I recognized the truth of this. I'd made progress but worried that my trip to Kiev might be a lapse and that I would be pulled back into my old life.

Marta met me at the airport. She had tied a small plastic orange strip to her bag and held roses in her hand, which she gave to me. We hugged.

"How great to see you," I told her. "Just like 1991."

"It's so much better!" she said. "Even Yurko is interested in politics now. Wait until you see the square."

Her apartment just about backed onto it. The din from protesters in the background when we spoke by phone had been so pronounced that I packed earplugs for both of us to help us with sleep.

Yurko, Marta's driver, flew an orange ribbon from his car antenna. As we approached, a fellow orange supporter honked at him; he honked right back. The radio blared through Yurko's rolled-up window glass. I heard the sound of Parliament in session. Once in the car, we honked our way through the parking lot, down the road and onto the Kiev-bound highway. "Even the border officer was nice," I told Marta. "He smiled when he stamped my passport."

Marta pointed out changes as we drove. Tall apartment buildings had sprouted by the highway. We flew past a large new supermarket, over a bridge that I knew well, the broad Dnipro coursing below. Yurko plotted a route that skirted closed roads. He found a back way into Marta's courtyard. We heard chanting from protesters in Independence Square. We dropped our bags and then walked half a block into the centre of the Orange Revolution. I could not believe my eyes.

"I've never seen anything like this," I shouted. Marta could not hear me. Rock bands played on stage. Their speakers blared. Cheers from fans filled all lulls. Marta and I linked arms and snaked our way through the crowd. I felt claustrophobic, remembering that sense of entrapment when Hungarian police in Budapest had appeared on motorcycles and fired tear gas during a demonstration.

Now, deep in this crowd, I could see no escape route. My view ahead was blocked by people's backs. I looked up at the sky, the one place that was still an empty space. Then I looked down again and fought claustrophobia. Marta and I were swept along in a sea of people. We soon found ourselves in the centre of the square. We faced a huge stage festooned with orange decorations.

So many popular bands played. We were as excited to hear them as everyone else in the crowd. Other people wore orange hats, orange scarves, orange jackets and orange mittens. If they had no orange clothes, they wore orange garbage bags with holes cut out for their arms, or tied orange ribbons around their wrists, foreheads or necks. Young guys danced on dumpsters.

"It's cool to be orange," I think Marta shouted. Each syllable was a puff of steam.

I only really heard the word *cool*. At minus 7 degrees Celsius, she might have meant the weather. Smoke wafted up from fires in huge metal bins. People huddled around the bins with their hands stretched out. I felt ice and snow crunch underfoot. From the excited look on Marta's face, I think I guessed right the first time, that she felt proud to see Ukrainians out in numbers like this.

We moved toward the street. I wanted to tell Marta how different this Ukraine was from the one that I had left, but she still could not hear me. I glanced over at tents that housed striking students. This tent city stretched down Khreshchatyk toward the Bessarabskyi Market and blocked all traffic. It seemed that half of Kiev filled the square. I remembered when students last camped here in 1990 and the one communications tool they had. It was that megaphone. Now digital cameras clicked and people swapped pictures and messages over cell phones. Ukraine had matured in many ways, but not in how it treated political opponents.

I was not prepared for the shock of seeing Victor Yushchenko. He came on stage to give a speech. He stood there, rigid. His face was ravaged. This punishment by poisoning – not yet proved but also doubted by no one – might even be worse than exile to the Gulag. I remembered what New York Marta, who still lived in Kiev, had told me. "Doctors inject painkillers into Yushchenko's spine," she said. "Every time he's on TV we try to see if he's getting better, but he still looks so bad."

As I stood there and watched Yushchenko speak, I agreed. I admired his courage and stamina. He thanked people for coming to the square and addressed army officers. "My friends," he said. He asked military men not to respond if the president declared a state of emergency and ordered the use of force. A student in front of me checked his phone. I saw his message. A contact sent him information on more pro-Yushchenko protests organized by students for the next day.

"How likely do you think it is there'll be a crackdown?" I asked Marta. She told me about a turning point a few days before I arrived when a military officer spoke in the square in support of Yushchenko. She also said, "some of the officers' wives and children are in the square. I don't think they'll shoot."

We had come home and now sat on the sofa in Marta's living room. I had been away for eight years, but her apartment still felt the same except for the sound of the window panes rattling from the noise in the square. The doorbell rang in the middle of our conversation. James arrived, then Stephen and finally Yaroslav. Time collapsed. All these friends from different periods, now scattered around the world, had come back to cover the protests. Everyone found a chair and worked.

James talked to his editor. Then he flipped through a magazine on Marta's side table.

"I'm going to Crimea. Do you want to come?" Yaroslav asked me. I did not want to go. That life of chasing news stories had passed. I had only features to write and the luxury of time. Yaroslav, as action-oriented and sharp-witted as ever, quietly planned his next scoop.

Stephen had come from London. We gossiped about old colleagues. There was no awkwardness in that gap of time that had passed. These friendships felt unchanged. Later, after everyone had left, I rummaged through my suitcase and handed Marta a package of earplugs.

"I'm not sure they'll work with all this racket," I said.

"You'll get used to it," Marta told me. I did not. Sleep was impossible, even with earplugs. At 2 a.m. I booted up my laptop and began work on assignments from my Toronto job.

During the day, Marta and I wandered. The Orange Revolution, headquartered on Khreshchatyk and in the square, reached far beyond these hubs, to all the main government and presidential offices. We walked up a cobblestone hill, toward the presidential administration. We passed a group of young guys dressed in orange smocks made from garbage bags. The hip-hop anthem of the revolution, "Together we are many; they will not defeat us," blared from their boom box. The music trailed behind us, then faded away as we turned right onto Bankova Street and saw riot police, who stood two rows deep. For several days protesters had blockaded ministerial and presidential offices, forcing the administration to work in exile from the outskirts of the city. These riot police had only recently arrived and now controlled the streets around the presidential administration, though the administration had not returned to Kiev.

I knew this neighbourhood well. A small pedestrian path down an embankment, just beyond where the riot police stood, led to my old address. I still thought of it as Karl Marx Street, even though it had been renamed Vulytsia Horodets'koho some time ago. I had wandered here on evening walks and admired the stately architecture, much of which pre-dated the 1917 revolution, when sugar barons lived in Kiev. Beyond the rows of riot police, I could see Horodetsky House, its art nouveau facade strewn with fantastic animal scenes, and the imposing white columned presidential administration across the street, the old Communist Party headquarters, where I had watched looters inside after Ukraine declared independence.

I thought again of Yushchenko's speech and his appeal to officers. I wondered about the possibility of conflict. The police kept their helmet visors up and their shields down, which was a good sign, for now. Three young women crossed a no man's land that separated bystanders like us and protesters from the police. The women held bright bouquets. They handed the flowers to the police officers.

"What did they say?" I asked Marta.

"They're begging the riot police not to harm anyone in the crowd." Orange balloons bobbed above the police barrier, held in place with shiny ribbon. Candles, flames flickering, stood on the pavement in front.

We strolled past tents pitched by the sidewalk and saw empty oil drums with fires inside that kept people warm. The Writer's Union across the road, an elegant yellow low-rise with a soup truck parked in front, was another headquarters for the Orange Revolution. Marta and I walked inside. Protesters in orange packed the ground-floor hallway. We followed a sign for the medical centre. Doctors wore plastic name tags. Garbage bags ringed the perimeter of the room. Donated clothes tumbled from the overstuffed bags.

"Do you need anything?" Marta asked one of the doctors.

"We have all this," the doctor said as he pointed at the bags of clothes, "but our medical supplies are low." Marta pulled out her notebook. The doctor dictated the names of drugs to buy – antibiotics, eye drops and many more things that I could not identify with my limited vocabulary.

We left the Writer's Union and walked down the road to a pharmacy. Its shelves spilled over with products. I read labels as Marta ordered stock. For thirty dollars we emerged with a bulging bag of medicine. I found it odd that nothing, not even antibiotics, required a prescription.

We returned to the medical centre at the Writer's Union and gave a doctor our bag of medicine. As we left, we passed by a staircase. People wrapped in blankets slept across every step – overflow from the designated first-floor rest area. When I looked in that room, I saw a sea of slumberers and no unoc-cupied chair. Sleeping bags and pillows blanketed the stage. Those who found no space on the stage lay on the floor.

We continued our walk. We took a back route, down a hill, to the top of Vulytsia Horodets'koho, crossed through a small park at the end of the street and climbed the footpath that led toward the president's office. At the top of the path, we encountered more riot police, grim-faced, clutching truncheons, in no mood to talk. Admitting defeat – we would not get closer to the building than this – we hovered for a few minutes, then went back down the path. We stopped briefly, riveted by a news broadcast on a small television. Several large-screen TVs, professionally installed, stood at strategic points in the city centre to keep protesters well informed of the news. This small black and white TV was not one of them. It balanced precariously on a metal structure. Wet snow fell. I felt amazed that no one had been electrocuted changing channels.

Yushchenko's rival and the man backed by the regime, Viktor Yanukovych, appeared now on TV. The program showed clips from a big meeting of his supporters in southeastern Ukraine, who threatened secession from Ukraine. One of the announcers said Yanukovych's wife, Ludmila, had addressed a rally of anti–Orange Revolution people outside. She said that Yushchenko supporters in the square in Kiev were so happy because they had eaten oranges imported from the U.S. laced with hallucinatory drugs.

People who stood near us gossiped about Mr. and Mrs. Yanukovych. I heard that Yanukovych had been jailed twice, for assault and then theft; Ludmila used to drive a trolleybus and Yanukovych, in the 1970s, drove racing cars in Monte Carlo; on their first date, a brick fell on Ludmila's head, Yanukovych rushed her to hospital and then proposed. I had no idea if any of this was true. All I knew was that they managed to stay married all those years. I had not.

In the evenings, I met with friends and caught up on their news. So many of my female friends were either thinking about divorce, in the middle of divorce, already divorced or single. I tried to tease wisdom from this observation but did not get far. We all loved to travel and had all worked as journalists, but the similarities in our circumstances ended there. I noticed some gender divide. Stephen, Yaroslav and James all remained married. I discussed this with Marta. Then, as always, with so much going on, our conversation drifted back to politics. The phone rang.

"It's for you," Marta said and handed me the receiver.

"Hi, it's me," Yaroslav said. "What are you doing for dinner?"

"Marta's busy, but I'm free," I told him. We arranged to meet at Yaroslav's hotel. A few minutes later Stephen telephoned. I invited him along.

I felt that I was walking into my past as I climbed the hill to meet Yaroslav. He was staying in an old Communist Party hotel where we had often eaten in 1990. Few other restaurants existed then in Kiev. I wondered how Yaroslav felt lodged in this hotel, like a visitor in his own home city. His life was so different from when he left.

I reached the hotel around 9 p.m. and rode up in the elevator with a man in his late thirties or early forties, who wore a bright orange down jacket. Heavy stubble covered his cheeks and chin. He had a scruffy air of authority.

Stephen arrived not long after me. We waited in Yaroslav's room while he filed his story. He spoke with his editor. I remembered this work rhythm so well and that sense of satisfaction with a story filed, the work day finished and dinner deserved. Much as I enjoyed reporting, I did not feel tempted to make this my life again. I still thought of my office in Toronto, worked on assignments for it and found time for writing to family, colleagues and friends back home.

When Yaroslav had finished, we took the elevator down to the hotel restaurant. This cavernous room was mostly empty. People crowded around one long table at the far end.

I recognized Volodymyr Filenko, a Member of Parliament and behind-the-scenes organizer for the Orange Revolution. The man with the orange jacket and a heavy-set male companion occupied another table. We sat at a table next to them. A few minutes later Stephen said, "Look, it's Yulia."

This woman, Yulia Tymoshenko, fascinated me. She and Yushchenko operated as a team. Yushchenko was the statesman. Yulia had drive and popular appeal, even though some people hated her and pointed to her questionable past in the gas industry. It had made her very rich. Slender Yulia was also beautiful. She rose to power as a deputy prime minister and was then briefly held in jail on charges of forging documents and smuggling gas but was released and cleared of the charges.

Yushchenko, the statesman, and Yulia were temperamentally so different that I could not understand how they even got along. But they were as good as married in the public eye as they fought together for new presidential elections.

I watched Yulia stride through the restaurant in a snug orange sweater. Her hair was tightly braided and wrapped around her head in her trademark halo hairdo. She exuded such energy. I imagined lightning might flash from Yulia at any moment. Fascinated, I stared as she visited the men at other tables. Then she sat with the man in the orange jacket at the table next to us. We all tried to eavesdrop. Yaroslav had the best spot for that.

When a crackdown had seemed imminent, Yulia helped inspire more protest. It had happened a few nights earlier. Marta and I returned home from a late dinner, astonished when we saw no people in the square. Our friend Nadezhda crossed it in the distance. We shouted out to her and met up in the centre.

"Yushchenko and Yulia told everyone to block the presidential administration and the Council of Ministers, so they all left," Nadezhda said.

Marta went home. Nadezhda and I investigated. We went on a midnight stroll to the presidential administration.

"Do you think Yulia's braid is real?" I asked Nadezhda as we walked up the hill.

"My friend's grandmother loves that braid. It reminds her of villages in the Carpathians," Nadezhda said. Neither of us could decide if the long blonde plait that Yulia wrapped around her head was real or a hairpiece. Near the top of the hill, we forgot about the braid, faced again with a massive crowd. As we penetrated farther into it, I saw no other women.

We pushed and jostled our way to the front of the crowd and reached a human blockade. It stretched one very long block deep, from the main intersection, down Bankova Street, past the Writer's Union to the presidential administration. Young guys stood, arms linked, stretched across the street, tens, if not hundreds of rows deep, illuminated by the yellow glow of streetlights.

"Let us through, we want to see what's happening," Nadezhda shouted at one of the guys.

He shook his head, "No one's allowed past."

"We're accredited journalists," Nadezhda insisted. She pulled out her press card.

The young man shook his head again, "It's too dangerous."

"What's going on?"

"The order's been given to send troops in," he said. I saw no troops, but this militant atmosphere and mood of grim determination signalled major change.

"Nadezhda!" someone shouted. We turned and saw six young guys, one a distant relative of hers, all from out of town and camped in her living room.

"Tell your friends to let us through," she fumed. They apologized but refused. The well-organized blockade held firm. Nadezhda relented.

We walked in the other direction, toward the Council of Ministers building, a few blocks away. I checked my watch under a streetlight – 1:25 a.m.

We heard drummers before we reached the building. They lined a leafy park embankment across the street. Their beat sounded like a celebration.

"Why is everyone so happy?" I asked a group of smiling young women outside the Council of Ministers building.

"They've pulled back the troops," one of them yelled over the sound of the drums. It was tense back there but a party here. I wondered whose information was correct.

One thin line of students guarded the building. I bumped into an American acquaintance who was still working in Kiev. Well-connected and a trustworthy source, she confirmed that troops had been pulled back.

In the morning, Marta and I woke late and rushed half a block down the road to the tent city. One of Marta's colleagues from the National University of the Kyiv-Mohyla Academy planned to let us in. Guards who surrounded the camp perimeter stopped us. They stood on slabs of Styrofoam, which insulated their feet from the cold. They dispatched a student to find Marta's colleague. She arrived and vouched for us. The guards stamped our hands and let us through.

The tent city was long and stretched down several blocks of Khreshchatyk. We entered the Kyiv-Mohyla section, near Independence Square. Students operated in shifts that lasted from three to ten hours. A donation of large tents had just arrived. Everyone discussed how best to pitch them and looked forward to better conditions.

"We'll be able to stand," one of the students enthused as we hunched close together under the low roof of a pup tent. "Heaters should fit inside." Already damp and a little chilled at minus 3 degrees Celsius, I became nearly as excited as him. As we left, a student who passed by us thrust squares of Styrofoam into our hands.

"Stand on them," he ordered Marta and me, "or else you'll come down with the flu." We moved on, handed our Styrofoam to a cold-looking nineteen-year-old, and then bumped into the cough drop and vitamin brigade.

"Please, save them for others, we're just visiting," I insisted. The two young women — more determined than us — shovelled cough drops and vitamins into our pockets and waited until we swallowed some.

"Illness is a big problem for us," Marta's colleague explained. "They're taking every precaution to keep people healthy."

"Only a dozen people showed up today," one of the students said. "Some of us have been out here for ten days. We're getting tired and sick. We need a break."

Others worried about falling behind in their studies. I thought of Senad in Sarajevo and how he had said the siege had cheated him of time. Corrupt as the election here might have been, I felt thankful these students would not face war.

As we spoke, I heard the clang of metal hitting pavement. I turned and saw a crew that shovelled garbage. Marta and I said goodbye and walked a short distance away from Independence Square, down Khreshchatyk and farther into the camp, in the direction of the Bessarabskyi Market. We met some young women outside a tent, who offered us tea and orange candies.

Refreshed, we continued our walk. We passed by a huge orange-coloured Christmas tree and a prayer tent that also contained sacks of food and then reached a building identified as command headquarters. A sign that said Do Not Enter was posted on it. We could go no farther, so we turned back and moved toward Independence Square. Soon we reached a Styrofoam wall.

"What's beyond this?" I asked one of the students.

"Headquarters for another section of the camp," he said. We had reached the end of Kyiv-Mohyla territory. It was well organized, with a military-like structure.

Marta and I were in her apartment when we heard the good news. She monitored TV broadcasts while I worked on Toronto assignments in the kitchen. She shouted, "Susan, they've done it. The Supreme Court ruled in favour of a repeat election."

"The square!" I yelled back. I had already pulled on my coat and boots.

"Go ahead without me," Marta said, scribbling furiously in her notebook, "I want to hear the rest of this newscast, then I'll join you."

I emerged from her courtyard into a street packed with people. One man beamed and then shouted "There is a God!" People streamed into the square. I joined them, buoyed by all the energy and excitement.

Somehow, Marta found me a short while later. We stood shoulder to shoulder as we were nearly the same height. We squeezed closer each minute as more people poured into the square. Soon no space remained and the adjacent streets were just as crammed. Yushchenko came on stage. He called the judges who issued the ruling "heroes."

"From today Ukraine is a democratic country," he said. People in the square roared. Everyone looked so proud. More people spoke. When darkness fell, fireworks illuminated the night sky, with bursts of colours that trailed down to the ground. Some reflected on faces turned toward the sky.

The next day I went for a walk to test the mood in the city. The square, so full this past week, was now nearly empty. I crossed through it to the post office on the other side of Khreshchatyk and entered a café inside the building. As I waited for coffee, I overheard a conversation between women about the outgoing president:

"He's sly," one of them said.

"He'll find a way of cheating Yushchenko again," her friend replied.

I left the café and walked down Khreshchatyk. The tent city still stretched down the street. It looked more entrenched than before. Young guys wove pieces of wood between wire to create a fence around the camp perimeter. I walked up the hill toward the presidential administration and found the atmosphere there more militant than on Khreshchatyk. Protesters blockaded the street with a checkpoint. Flags fluttered in the breeze. They raised a rickety homemade barrier so some cars could pass but blocked others. Tents multiplied, the air even smokier now from more fires in metal drums. Even though the court had ruled in favour of Yushchenko, these protesters still expected they might be tricked. They said they would not go home until new elections had been held.

They would not relax, but I did now. I took a day off to visit Mary's riding club. We passed near a wealthy enclave as we drove out to the club. "That's where the presidential administration is holed up," Mary said.

I had heard about this suburb of columned and turreted mansions along with rumours about the dubious wealth that funded it. I lost track of all the allegations of money laundering, bribes, twisted tax laws and mafia involvement.

"They're building castles on sand," Mary told me. Apparently some land in this area was not stable enough to support houses planned for it.

In the evening, Mary and I met Toronto Marta, New York Marta, Nadezhda and other friends for dinner in a restaurant. We sat on wooden chairs. Heaps of varenykyi, Chicken Kiev, mushroom starters and wine stood on the polished wood table. After a few glasses, Mary shouted, "Let's call Bill!" Someone dialed his number. He answered, surprised by the call.

"Bill, you should be here!" Mary said.

"I can't. I've got responsibilities now," he replied. I thought of Bill in London, where we had last met. I understood that he'd moved on.

I had as well. I no longer questioned where I belonged. Toronto was my home. But just now I felt somewhere in between. This unexpected meeting up with so many old friends reminded me of past lives in Kiev and London and other places too. So many memories that I had shut away now tumbled out.

I went for a walk in my old neighbourhood. I felt drawn first to Yaroslaviv Val and the building where I fled the man who rang my doorbell all night long. I remembered its genteel shabbiness, apartment buildings that crumbled and potholed roads. I climbed the hill, reached my old building and pinched myself twice in case this was a dream. Then I checked the street address. Was I mistaken? Could this building that looked plucked from central Paris be where I had lived? I scrutinized the facelift, the impeccably painted trim, lights positioned to accentuate architectural details and realized that it was my old building.

Half in a daze, recognizing where I stood but disoriented by such change, I wandered down the street and passed the building where I had lived with Natalia Ivanovna and Ira. I stepped into the courtyard. Then I hesitated. I wanted to go up and ring the bell but did not. Some memories were best left alone.

Once I was back on the street, I peered in the plate-glass windows of shops that displayed elegant patisseries. Then I strolled into Saint Sophia's Square. I remembered an outbreak of violence in the square just before I left Ukraine. Members of one religious denomination had wanted to bury the head of their church, who had recently died, on the cathedral's grounds. Barred from entry by the police, they dug up the pavement in front of St. Sophia's and buried their leader underneath. Fur-clad women now strolled along the sidewalk near the cathedral and browsed in a Vivienne Westwood boutique.

My time in Kiev passed quickly. A few days before I was due to leave, I joined Marta for a talk by a well known professor from Oxford, Timothy Garton Ash, who had recently flown in. We sat with Ukrainian students on wooden chairs in a Kyiv-Mohyla classroom as he analyzed the Orange Revolution. I listened, amazed by his ability to bundle events still unfolding into a tidy theoretical framework. Professor Garton Ash told students the Orange Revolution had transformed Ukraine's image in the West, but he also said that even though European states applauded the Orange Revolution, the European Union would not (at least not soon) offer Ukraine membership.

"Poland is for us," someone shouted from the back of the room. The professor said that was not enough. Then he warned that criminals would not be "called to account." Ukrainians could expect truth, not justice. I wondered about this last point.

After the lecture, Marta stayed at the university. I wanted to buy presents for people at home. I walked back to a souvenir shop on Khreshchatyk where I might find *pysanky* – Ukrainian Easter eggs. I had received my first one from a high school friend before I even knew Ukraine existed. She didn't either. We both just marvelled at this beautiful, intricately painted egg and wondered who had made it.

The shop was located on the ground floor of the Union of Journalists building. As I approached, I noticed a small memorial plaque on a wall. I stopped and read the plaque. To my surprise, it listed the names of journalists who had died under suspicious circumstances. I checked each letter twice to be certain that I made no mistake about the first name there. Vadym Boyko. He had made the list and was not forgotten, though his murder had never been solved. This still upset me and I was sure it always would, but I did feel happy to see this plaque commemorating Vadym and other colleagues.

I thought of Vadym as I browsed in the store. Distracted, I left empty-handed. I walked back down Khreshchatyk, up a steep hill toward St. Sophia's Cathedral and over to Andrivskyi Spusk. The walk cleared my mind and returned me to the present. I browsed souvenir stalls that lined the street for *pysanky*.

I would have a dinner date when I returned to Toronto with someone who made my heart flutter. I thought of him now and bought him an egg. Two finely painted roosters surrounded by geometric designs decorated the shell. He was not Ukrainian, so he might not know about these eggs, but it meant a lot to me to give him one. I had my own collection and had carried each piece home by hand. As I stood on one of the earliest streets in Kiev with my *pysanka,* a painted egg first made in ancient times, I realized again how much older this culture was than mine. I returned through St. Sophia's Square to Khreshchatyk. I passed by the tent city, where protesters still held signs for free and fair elections. They would come soon I knew, but this democracy would be a fragile one. As with my egg, too much pressure might crack a hollow shell. But for now, it was something beautiful to watch.

ACKNOWLEDGMENTS

Thanks for friendship, shared adventures and help with the manuscript to Anna, Charlotte, James, Katya, New York Marta, Roma, Sallie, Stephen, Toronto Marta and Yaroslav. Helga, Sabine and Ute (all pseudonyms), you will recognize yourselves if you read this book. I hope that we will meet again some day.

I am lucky to have caring relatives and friends who did so much for me after my cycling accident. Thank you to Rachel Morgan, Anne and John Morse Jones, Martin Morse Jones, Eirian and John James, and to my late cousin Alyson James, whose kindness I will always remember. Thanks also to Jennifer Cowell and Dr. Jean Staffurth, as well as to the wonderful doctors and nurses on the University College Hospital orthopaedics ward. Jonathan Cohen, Charles Erin, Sabina McGarrahan, Michelle Oakes and Celia Russell were all good friends in London.

For giving me a start in journalism, I am grateful to Nick Thorpe, Valerie Carter, George Schöpflin, the *Guardian* foreign desk, and especially Steve Crawshaw at the *Independent*, whose support was essential for moving to Soviet Ukraine. Thank you to Liz Robson and David Morton at the BBC for returning me to London and to Leonard Doyle at the *Independent on Sunday*, who welcomed me back in 2004 after such a long absence, to cover the Orange Revolution.

In Budapest, I lived through exciting times and shared good memories with many people, including Ernest Beck, Nick Denton, Laszlo Egyed, Peter Futo, Ildiko Kemeny, Michael Kuttner, Jutka Szombat, the Simaly and Vertesy families, Gabor Xantos and Zoltan Zarandy.

The same is true in Ukraine for Volodya Ariyev, Marta Baziuk, Luda Beletskaia, Greta Bull, Natalka Feduschak, Chrystia Freeland, Marga Hewko, Yurko Holianych, Matthew Kaminski, Chrystia Lapychak, Irene Marushko, Lida Poletz, Bob Seely, Sasha Stetsenko, Slava and Tanya, Alex Shprintsen, Oleksander Tkachenko, Constance Uzwhyshyn and Mykola Veresen.

Karen Connelly launched me on the way to this book when she reviewed a chapter as writer-in-residence at the Toronto Reference Library. She also introduced me to Kelly Dignan, a very talented editor. *Picnic at the Iron Curtain* is almost as much Kelly's as mine. Her insightful comments helped so much in shaping it. My sister, Deborah Viets, was equally skilled in finessing sentences and catching errors, but I owe more to her than this. I have always respected her judgment the most. She gave me the confidence to persevere when she read a chapter and liked it.

My family has helped in so many other ways. My parents always encouraged me to take risks and explore. I am even more grateful for this in retrospect than I was during all those years away from Canada. I realize now they let me go when many other parents might have held their children back. When I did return to Canada for visits, my brother, Mark, met me at the airport. Once I saw his face at the arrivals gate, I felt that I had truly arrived home.

I remember with warmth and love my late mother-in-law, Sakina Mitta, who read and commented on many chapters and was a wonderful, wise companion and a role model for aging. Finally, to my husband, Aamer, thank you for all your help along the way and even more for the happiness that has made life at home so good and writing this book so much fun.

SOURCES

Bennett, Will. "Blood-feud tradition claims innocent life." *Independent*, May 2, 1994.

Bowcott, Owen and David Pallister. "Caucasus feud spills into Surrey." *Guardian*, May 2, 1994.

Burrell, Ian. "Chechen's justice hits Willow Way – Killing in Woking." *Sunday Times*, May 8, 1994.

Guardian, "'The idea was to put me as a victim,' he said before he killed himself – Chechenia murder," October 22, 1993.

Hanley, Charles J. "On warlords' wish list: 22 pounds of shoulder-fired lightning." Associated Press, November 20, 1993.

Hanley, Charles J. "The quest for the Stinger. It's a 'nightmare weapon' if it gets into the hands of drug dealers, terrorists. CIA trying to buy back missiles shipped to Afghanistan guerillas." Associated Press, February 13, 1994.

MacKinnon, Ian. "Professional hitman blamed for murder." *Independent*, May 2, 1994.

Reuters News, "Armenian jailed for life for political killings," October 21, 1993.

Reuters News, "Court told Armenian KGB ordered Russians' murder," October 18, 1993.

Tendler, Stewart. "Suburban murder trail leads back to KGB assassinations." *Times*, May 2, 1994.

Thompson, Tony. "Russian gangsters target UK." *Observer*, February 11, 2001.

Times, "Prisoner questioned – murder of Karen Reed," May 4, 1994.

Weale, Sally. "Russian pair 'executed in penthouse.'" *Guardian*, October 14, 1993.